Image of Excellence

Wisdom and Inspiration for Today's Businesswoman

D1506931

Image of Excellence

Wisdom and Inspiration
for Today's Businesswoman

Tulsa, Oklahoma

Unless otherwise indicated, all Scripture quotations are taken from the *King James Version* of the Bible.

2nd Printing
Over 25,000 in Print

Image of Excellence —
Wisdom and Inspiration
for Today's Businesswoman
ISBN 1-56292-005-7
Copyright © 1992 by Honor Books
P. O. Box 55388
Tulsa, Oklahoma 74155-1388

CONTENTS

THE VIRTUOUS WOMAN

Who can find a virtuous woman? for her price is far above rubies. The heart of her husband doth safely trust in her, so that he shall have no need of spoil. She will do him good and not evil all the days of her life.

She seeketh wool, and flax, and worketh willingly with her hands. She is like the merchants' ships; she bringeth her food from afar.

She riseth while it is yet night, and giveth meat to her maidens. She considereth a field and buyeth it: with the fruit of her hands she planteth a vineyard.

She girdeth her loins with strength, and strengtheneth her arms. She perceiveth that her merchandise is good: her candle goeth not out by night.

She layeth her hands to the spindle, and her hands hold the distaff. She stretcheth out her

11

hand to the poor; yea, she reacheth forth her hands to the needy.

She is not afraid of the snow for her household: for all her household are clothed with scarlet. She maketh herself coverings of tapestry; her clothing is silk and purple.

Her husband is known in the gates when he sitteth among the elders of the land.

She maketh fine linen, and selleth it; and delivereth girdles unto the merchant. Strength and honour are her clothing; and she shall rejoice in time to come.

She openeth her mouth with wisdom; and in her tongue is the law of kindness. She looketh well to the ways of her household, and eateth not the bread of idleness.

Her children arise up, and call her blessed; her husband also, and he praiseth her. Many daughters have done virtuously, but thou excellest them all.

Favour is deceitful, and beauty is vain: but a woman that feareth the Lord, she shall be praised. Give her of the fruit of her hands; and let her own works praise her in the gates.

Proverbs 31:10-31

Image of Excellence

Wisdom and Inspiration
for Today's Businesswoman

PART I
WISDOM AND COMFORT
THROUGH THE SCRIPTURES

1
THE BUSINESSWOMAN AND HER ATTITUDE

The Faith of A Businesswoman

And they that know thy name will put their trust in thee: for thou, Lord, hast not forsaken them that seek thee.

Psalm 9:10

Trust in the Lord, and do good; so shalt thou dwell in the land, and verily thou shalt be fed.
Delight thyself also in the Lord; and he shall give thee the desires of thine heart.
Commit thy way unto the Lord; trust also in him; and he shall bring it to pass.

Psalm 37:3-5

Thou wilt keep him in perfect peace, whose mind is stayed on thee: because he trusteth in thee.

Isaiah 26:3

Blessed is the man that trusteth in the Lord, and whose hope the Lord is.

Jeremiah 17:7

And when he was come into the house, the blind men came to him: and Jesus saith unto them, Believe ye that I am able to do this? They said unto him, Yea, Lord.

Then touched he their eyes, saying, According to your faith be it unto you.

Matthew 9:28,29

And Jesus said unto them, Because of your unbelief: for verily I say unto you, If ye have faith as a grain of mustard seed, ye shall say unto this mountain, Remove hence to yonder place; and it shall remove; and nothing shall be impossible unto you.

Matthew 17:20

And all things, whatsoever ye shall ask in prayer, believing, ye shall receive.

Matthew 21:22

Jesus said unto him, If thou canst believe, all things are possible to him that believeth.

Mark 9:23

And Jesus answering saith unto them, Have faith in God.

For verily I say unto you, That whosoever shall say unto this mountain, Be thou removed, and be thou cast into the sea; and shall not doubt in his heart, but shall believe that those things which he saith shall come to pass; he shall have whatsoever he saith.

Therefore I say unto you, What things so ever ye desire, when ye pray, believe that ye receive them, and ye shall have them.

Mark 11:22-24

So then faith cometh by hearing, and hearing by the word of God.

Romans 10:17

For I say, through the grace given unto me, to every man that is among you, not to think of himself more highly than he ought to think; but to think soberly, according as God hath dealt to every man the measure of faith.

Romans 12:3

Above all, taking the shield of faith, where with ye shall be able to quench all the fiery darts of the wicked.

Ephesians 6:16

Cast not away therefore your confidence, which hath great recompence of reward.

Hebrews 10:35

Now faith is the substance of things hoped for, the evidence of things not seen.

But without faith it is impossible to please him: for he that cometh to God must believe that he is, and that he is a rewarder of them that diligently seek him.

Hebrews 11:1,6

Looking unto Jesus the author and finisher of our faith; who for the joy that was set before him endured the cross, despising the shame, and is set down at the right hand of the throne of God.

Hebrews 12:2

Let your conversation be without covetousness and be content with such things as ye have: for he hath said, I will never leave thee, nor forsake thee.

So that we may boldly say, The Lord is my helper, and I will not fear what man shall do unto me.

Hebrews 13:5,6

And the prayer of faith shall save the sick, and the Lord shall raise him up; and if he have committed sins, they shall be forgiven him.

James 5:15

That the trial of your faith, being much more precious than of gold that perisheth, though it be tried with fire, might be found unto praise and honour and glory at the appearing of Jesus Christ:

Whom having not seen, ye love; in whom, though now ye see him not, yet believing, ye rejoice with joy unspeakable and full of glory:

Receiving the end of your faith, even the salvation of your souls.

1 Peter 1:7-9

For whatsoever is born of God overcometh the world: and this is the victory that overcometh the world, even our faith.

1 John 5:4

The Motivation of a Businesswoman

Be strong and of a good courage, fear not, nor be afraid of them: for the Lord thy God, he it is that doth go with thee; he will not fail thee, nor forsake thee.

Deuteronomy 31:6

Be strong and of a good courage: for unto this people shalt thou divide for an inheritance the land, which I sware unto their fathers to give them.

Joshua 1:6

For the Lord hath driven out from before you great nations and strong: but as for you, no man hath been able to stand before you unto this day.

Joshua 23:9

And David was greatly distressed; for the people spake of stoning him, because the soul of all the people was grieved, every man for his sons and for his daughters: but David encouraged himself in the Lord his God.

1 Samuel 30:6

And he answered, Fear not: for they that be with us are more than they that be with them.

2 Kings 6:16

Through thee will we push down our enemies: through thy name will we tread them under that rise up against us.

Psalm 44:5

Give instruction to a wise man, and he will be yet wiser: teach a just man, and he will increase in learning.

Proverbs 9:9

By much slothfulness the building decayeth and through idleness of the hands the house droppeth through.

Ecclesiastes 10:18

For I the Lord thy God will hold thy right hand, saying unto thee, Fear not; I will help thee.

Isaiah 41:13

And they that be wise shall shine as the brightness of the firmament; and they that turn many to righteousness as the stars for ever and ever.

Daniel 12:3

Ask, and it shall be given you; seek, and ye shall find; knock, and it shall be opened unto you:

For every one that asketh receiveth; and he that seeketh findeth; and to him that knocketh it shall be opened.

Matthew 7:7,8

And I say also unto thee, That thou art Peter, and upon this rock I will build my church; and the gates of hell shall not prevail against it.

And I will give unto thee the keys of the kingdom of heaven: and whatsoever thou shalt bind on earth shall be bound in heaven: and whatsoever thou shalt loose on earth shall be loosed in heaven.

Matthew 16:18,19

Verily, verily, I say unto you, He that believeth on me, the works that I do shall he do also; and greater works than these shall he do; because I go unto my Father.

John 14:12

But ye shall receive power, after that the Holy Ghost is come upon you: and ye shall be witnesses unto me both in Jerusalem, and in all Judaea, and in Samaria, and unto the uttermost part of the earth.

Acts 1:8

For the weapons of our warfare are not carnal, but mighty through God to the pulling down of strongholds.

2 Corinthians 10:4

Wherefore he saith, Awake thou that sleepest, and arise from the dead, and Christ shall give thee light.

Ephesians 5:14

I can do all things through Christ which strengtheneth me.

Philippians 4:13

If God be for us who can be against us?

Romans 8:31

Strengthened with all might, according to his glorious power, unto all patience and long suffering with joyfulness.

Colossians 1:11

Walk in wisdom toward them that are without, redeeming the time.

Colossians 4:5

Meditate upon these things; give thyself wholly to them; that thy profiting may appear to all.

1 Timothy 4:15

Therefore leaving the principles of the doctrine of Christ, let us go on unto perfection.

Hebrews 6:1a

Ye are of God, little children, and have overcome them: because greater is he that is in you, than he that is in the world.

We are of God: he that knoweth God heareth us; he that is not of God heareth not us. Hereby know we the spirit of truth, and the spirit of error.

And we have known and believed the love that God hath to us. God is love; and he that dwelleth in love dwelleth in God, and God in him.

Herein is our love made perfect, that we may have boldness in the day of judgment: because as he is, so are we in this world.

1 John 4:4,6,16,17

Beloved, I wish above all things that thou mayest prosper and be in health, even as thy soul prospereth.

3 John 2

The Integrity of a Businesswoman

And if thou wilt walk before me, as David thy father walked, in integrity of heart, and in uprightness, to do according to all that I have commanded thee, and wilt keep my statutes and my judgments.

1 Kings 9:4

Let me be weighed in an even balance that God may know mine integrity.

Job 31:6

Blessed is the man that walketh not in the counsel of the ungodly, nor standeth in the way of sinners, nor sitteth in the seat of the scornful.

But his delight is in the law of the Lord; and in his law doth he meditate day and night.

Psalm 1:1,2

All the paths of the Lord are mercy and truth unto such as keep his covenant and his testimonies.

Let integrity and uprightness preserve me; for I wait on thee.

Psalm 25:10,21

Judge me, O Lord; for I have walked in mine integrity: I have trusted also in the Lord; therefore I shall not slide.

Psalm 26:1

And as for me, thou upholdest me in mine integrity, and settest me before thy face for ever.

Psalm 41:12

So he fed them according to the integrity of his heart; and guided them by the skilfulness of his hands.

Psalm 78:72

A good man sheweth favour, and lendeth: he will guide his affairs with discretion.

Psalm 112:5

Blessed are they that keep his testimonies, and that seek him with the whole heart.

Thou hast commanded us to keep thy precepts diligently.

Psalm 119:2,4

A false balance is abomination to the Lord: but a just weight is his delight.

The integrity of the upright shall guide them: but the perverseness of transgressors shall destroy them.

Proverbs 11:1,3

Better is a little with righteousness than great revenues without right.

Proverbs 16:8

Better is the poor that walketh in his integrity, than he that is perverse in his lips, and is a fool.

He that keepeth the commandment keepeth his own soul; but he that despiseth his ways shall die.

Proverbs 19:1,16

The just man walketh in his integrity: his children are blessed after him.

Proverbs 20:7

The getting of treasures by a lying tongue is a vanity tossed to and fro of them that seek death.

Proverbs 21:6

If ye be willing and obedient, ye shall eat the good of the land.

Isaiah 1:19

Recompense to no man evil for evil. Provide things honest in the sight of all men.

Romans 12:17

Wise Counsel and the Businesswoman

Blessed is the man that walketh not in the counsel of the ungodly, nor standeth in the way of sinners, nor sitteth in the seat of the scornful.

But his delight is in the law of the Lord; and in his law doth he meditate day and night.

And he shall be like a tree planted by the rivers of water, that bringeth forth his fruit in his season; his leaf also shall not wither; and whatsoever he doeth shall prosper.

Psalm 1:1,2,3

I will bless the Lord, who hath given me counsel: my reins also instruct me in the night seasons.

Psalm 16:7

Shew me thy ways, O Lord; teach me thy paths.

Psalm 25:4

One thing have I desired of the Lord, that will I seek after; that I may dwell in the house of the Lord all the days of my life, to behold the beauty of the Lord, and to inquire in his temple.

For in the time of trouble he shall hide me in his pavilion: in the secret of his tabernacle shall he hide me; he shall set me up upon a rock.

Psalm 27:3-5

I will instruct thee and teach thee in the way which thou shalt go: I will guide thee with mine eye.

Psalm 32:8

God is our refuge and strength, a very present help in trouble.

Psalm 46:1

Behold, thou desirest truth in the inward parts: and in the hidden part thou shalt make me to know wisdom.

Psalm 51:6

I will say of the Lord, He is my refuge and my fortress: my God; in him will I trust.

Psalm 91:2

Unto the upright there ariseth light in the darkness: he is gracious, and full of compassion, and righteous.

Psalm 112:4

The Lord is on my side; I will not fear: what can man do unto me?

It is better to trust in the Lord than to put confidence in man.

Psalm 118:6,8

For ever, O Lord, thy word is settled in heaven.

Psalm 119:89

For the Lord giveth wisdom: out of his mouth cometh knowledge and understanding.

Proverbs 2:6

Trust in the Lord with all thine heart; and lean not unto thine own understanding.

In all thy ways acknowledge him, and he shall direct thy paths.

Proverbs 3:5,6

My son, attend to my words; incline thine ear unto my sayings.

Let them not depart from thine eyes; keep them in the midst of thine heart.

For they are life unto those that find them, and health to all their flesh.

Proverbs 4:20-22

Where no counsel is, the people fall: but in the multitude of counsellors there is safety.

Proverbs 11:14

Without counsel purposes are disappointed: but in the multitude of counsellors they are established.

Proverbs 15:22

Ointment and perfume rejoice the heart: so doth the sweetness of a man's friend by hearty counsel.

Proverbs 27:9

And thine ears shall hear a word behind thee, saying, This is the way, walk ye in it, when ye turn to the right hand, and when ye turn to the left.

Isaiah 30:21

The grass withereth, the flower fadeth: but the word of our God shall stand for ever.

Isaiah 40:8

And I will bring the blind by a way that they knew not; I will lead them in paths that they have not known: I will make darkness light before them, and crooked things straight. These things will I do unto them, and not forsake them.

Isaiah 42:16

Thus saith the Lord, thy Redeemer, the Holy One of Israel; I am the Lord thy God which teacheth thee to profit, which leadeth thee by the way that thou shouldest go.

Isaiah 48:17

Heaven and earth shall pass away, but my words shall not pass away.

Matthew 24:34

Howbeit when he, the Spirit of truth, is come, he will guide you into all truth: for he shall not speak of himself; but whatsoever he shall hear, that shall he speak: and he will shew you things to come.

He shall glorify me: for he shall receive of mine, and shall shew it unto you.

John 16:13,14

What shall we then say to these things? If God be for us, who can be against us?

Romans 8:31

If any of you lack wisdom, let him ask of God, that giveth to all men liberally, and upbraideth not; and it shall be given him.

James 1:5

2
THE BUSINESSWOMAN AND HER CAREER

Helping an Employee Who Is Hurting

The Lord God hath given me the tongue of the learned, that I should know how to speak a word in season to him that is weary: he wakeneth morning by morning, he wakeneth mine ear to hear as the learned.

Isaiah 50:4

Is it not to deal thy bread to the hungry, and that thou bring the poor that are cast out to thy house? when thou seest the naked, that thou cover him; and that thou hide not thy self from thine own flesh?

Isaiah 58:7

Therefore all things whatsoever ye would that men should do to you, do ye even so to them: for this is the law and the prophets.

Matthew 7:12

And the second is like unto it, Thou shalt love thy neighbour as thyself.

Matthew 22:39

Then shall the King say unto them on his right hand, Come, ye blessed of my Father, inherit the kingdom prepared for you from the foundation of the world:

For I was an hungred, and ye gave me meat: I was thirsty, and ye gave me drink: I was a stranger, and ye took me in:

Naked, and ye clothed me: I was sick, and ye visited me: I was in prison, and ye came unto me.

Matthew 25:34-36

By this shall all men know that ye are my disciples, if ye have love one to another.

John 13:35

I have shewed you all things, how that so labouring ye ought to support the weak, and to remember the words of the Lord Jesus, how he said, It is more blessed to give than to receive.

Acts 20:35

Rejoice with them that do rejoice, and weep with them that weep.

Romans 12:15

We then that are strong ought to bear the infirmities of the weak, and not to please ourselves.

Romans 15:1

Blessed be God, even the Father of our Lord Jesus Christ, the Father of mercies, and the God of all comfort;

Who comforteth us in all our tribulation, that we may be able to comfort them which are in any trouble, by the comfort wherewith we ourselves are comforted of God.

For as the sufferings of Christ abound in us, so our consolation also aboundeth by Christ.

2 Corinthians 1:3-5

Bear ye one another's burdens, and so fulfil the law of Christ.

Galatians 6:2

Remember them that are in bonds, as bound with them; and them which suffer adversity, as being yourselves also in the body.

But to do good and to communicate forget not: for with such sacrifices God is well pleased.

Hebrews 13:3,16

If ye fulfil the royal law according to the scripture, Thou shalt love thy neighbour as thyself, ye do well.

James 2:8

Finally, be ye all of one mind, having compassion one of another, love as brethren, be pitiful, be courteous.

1 Peter 3:8

When Faced With Terminating an Employee

The Lord lift up his countenance upon thee, and give thee peace.

Numbers 6:26

(For the Lord thy God is a merciful God;) he will not forsake thee, neither destroy thee, nor forget the covenant of thy fathers which he sware unto them.

Deuteronomy 4:31

Be strong and of a good courage, fear not, nor be afraid of them: for the Lord thy God, he it is that doth go with thee; he will not fail thee, nor forsake thee.

And the Lord, he it is that doth go before thee; he will be with thee, he will not fail thee, neither forsake thee: fear not, neither be dismayed.

Deuteronomy 31:6,8

I had fainted, unless I had believed to see the goodness of the Lord in the land of the living.

Wait on the Lord: be of good courage, and he shall strengthen thine heart: wait, I say, on the Lord.

Psalm 27:13,14

Make thy face to shine upon thy servant: save me for thy mercies' sake.

Psalm 31:16

I have been young, and now am old; yet have I not seen the righteous forsaken, nor his seed begging bread.

Psalm 37:25

Therefore I say unto you, Take no thought for your life, what ye shall eat, or what ye shall drink; nor yet for your body, what ye shall put on. Is not the life more than meat, and the body than raiment?

Take therefore no thought for the morrow: for the morrow shall take thought for the things of itself. Sufficient unto the day is the evil thereof.

Matthew 6:25,34

Now the God of hope fill you with all joy and peace in believing, that ye may abound in hope, through the power of the Holy Ghost.

Romans 15:13

There hath no temptation taken you but such as is common to man: but God is faithful, who will not suffer you to be tempted above that ye are able; but will with the temptation also make a way to escape, that ye may be able to bear it.

1 Corinthians 10:13

Finally, my brethren, be strong in the Lord, and in the power of his might.

Ephesians 6:10

Not that I speak in respect of want: for I have learned, in whatsoever state I am, therewith to be content.

I know both how to be abased, and I know how to abound: every where and in all things I am instructed both to be full and to be hungry, both to abound and to suffer need.

I can do all things through Christ which strengtheneth me.

But my God shall supply all your need according to his riches in glory by Christ Jesus.

Philippians 4:11-13,19

I will never leave thee, nor forsake thee.

Hebrews 13:5B

That the trial of your faith, being much more precious than of gold that perisheth, though it be tried with fire, might be found unto praise and honour and glory at the appearing of Jesus Christ.

1 Peter 1:7

Casting all your care upon him; for he careth for you.

1 Peter 5:7

Dealing With Betrayal at Work

Teach me thy way, O Lord, and lead me in a plain path, because of mine enemies.

Wait on the Lord: be of good courage, and he shall strengthen thine heart: wait, I say, on the Lord.

Psalm 27:11,14

For I have heard the slander of many: fear was on every side: while they took counsel together against me, they devised to take away my life.

My times are in thy hand: deliver me from the hand of mine enemies, and from them that persecute me.

Make thy face to shine upon thy servant: save me for thy mercies' sake.

Psalm 31:13,15,16

The angel of the Lord encampeth round about them that fear him, and delivereth them.

O taste and see that the Lord is good: blessed is the man that trusteth in him.

Psalm 34:7,8

False witnesses did rise up; they laid to my charge things that I knew not.

They rewarded me evil for good to the spoiling of my soul.

But as for me, when they were sick, my clothing was sackcloth: I humbled my soul with fasting; and my prayer returned into mine own bosom.

I behaved myself as though he had been my friend or brother: I bowed down heavily, as one that mourneth for his mother.

But in mine adversity they rejoiced, and gathered themselves together: yea, the abjects gathered themselves together against me, and I knew it not; they did tear me, and ceased not:

Let not them that are mine enemies wrongfully rejoice over me: neither let them wink with the eye that hate me without a cause.

For they speak not peace: but they devise deceitful matters against them that are quiet in the land.

This thou hast seen, O Lord: keep not silence: O Lord, be not far from me.

Psalm 35:11-15,19,20,22

Yea, mine own familiar friend, in whom I trusted, which did eat of my bread, hath lifted up his heel against me.

But thou, O Lord, be merciful unto me, and raise me up, that I may requite them.

By this I know that thou favourest me, because mine enemy doth not triumph over me.

Psalm 41:9-11

For it was not an enemy that reproached me; then I could have borne it: neither was it he that hated me that did magnify himself against me; then I would have hid myself from him:

But it was thou, a man mine equal, my guide, and mine acquaintance.

We took sweet counsel together, and walked unto the house of God in company.

Psalm 55:12-14

He shall cover thee with his feathers, and under his wings shalt thou trust: his truth shall be thy shield and buckler.

Thou shalt not be afraid for the terror by night; nor for the arrow that flieth by day.

Psalm 91:4,5

A faithful witness will not lie: but a false witness will utter lies.

Proverbs 14:5

For the Lord God will help me; therefore shall I not be confounded: therefore have I set my face like a flint, and I know that I shall not be ashamed.

He is near that justifieth me; who will contend with me? let us stand together: who is mine adversary? let him come near to me.

Behold, the Lord God will help me; who is he that shall condemn me? lo, they all shall wax old as a garment; the moth shall eat them up.

Isaiah 50:7-9

Rejoice not against me, O mine enemy: when I fall, I shall arise; when I sit in darkness, the Lord shall be a light unto me.

Micah 7:8

Then one of the twelve, called Judas Iscariot, went unto the chief priests,

And said unto them, What will ye give me, and I will deliver him unto you? And they covenanted with him for thirty pieces of silver.

And from that time he sought opportunity to betray him.

Then cometh he to his disciples, and saith unto them, Sleep on now, and take your rest: behold, the hour is at hand, and the Son of man is betrayed into the hands of sinners.

Matthew 26:14-16,45

Let all bitterness, and wrath, and anger, and clamour, and evil speaking, be put away from you, with all malice.

Ephesians 4:31

Notwithstanding the Lord stood with me, and strengthened me; that by me the preaching might be fully known, and that all the Gentiles might hear: and I was delivered out of the mouth of the lion.

2 Timothy 4:17

Having a good conscience; that, whereas they speak evil of you, as of evil doers, they may be ashamed that falsely accuse your good conversation in Christ.

1 Peter 3:16

When Your Business Depends on You Alone

Be strong and of a good courage, fear not, nor be afraid of them: for the Lord thy God, he it is that doth go with thee; he will not fail thee, nor forsake thee.

Deuteronomy 31:6

Be ye strong therefore, and let not your hands be weak: for your work shall be rewarded.

2 Chronicles 15:7

Be of good courage, and he shall strengthen your heart, all ye that hope in the Lord.

Psalm 31:24

I will instruct thee and teach thee in the way which thou shalt go: I will guide thee with mine eye.

Psalm 32:8

Thou shalt guide me with thy counsel, and afterward receive me to glory.

Psalm 73:24

A good man sheweth favour, and lendeth: he will guide his affairs with discretion.

Psalm 112:5

For the Lord giveth wisdom: out of his mouth cometh knowledge and understanding.

Proverbs 2:6

Trust in the Lord with all thine heart; and lean not unto thine own understanding.

Proverbs 3:5

Counsel is mine, and sound wisdom: I am understanding; I have strength.

Proverbs 8:14

Seest thou a man diligent in his business? he shall stand before kings; he shall not stand before mean men.

Proverbs 22:29

Fear thou not; for I am with thee: be not dismayed; for I am thy God: I will strengthen thee; yea, I will help thee; yea, I will uphold thee with the right hand of my righteousness.

Isaiah 41:10

The Lord God is my strength, and he will make my feet like hinds' feet, and he will make me to walk upon mine high places.

Habakkuk 3:19

But seek ye first the kingdom of God, and his righteousness; and all these things shall be added unto you.

Matthew 6:33

And God is able to make all grace abound toward you; that ye, always having all sufficiency in all things, may abound to every good work.

2 Corinthians 9:8

Now unto him that is able to do exceeding abundantly above all that we ask or think, according to the power that worketh in us.

Ephesians 3:20

I can do all things through Christ which strengtheneth me.

Philippians 4:13

Cast not away therefore your confidence, which hath great recompence of reward.

For ye have need of patience, that, after ye have done the will of God, ye might receive the promise.

Hebrews 10:35-36

If any of you lack wisdom, let him ask of God, that giveth to all men liberally, and upbraideth not; and it shall be given him.

James 1:5

When Business Is Insufficient To Continue Operations

But if from thence thou shalt seek the Lord thy God, thou shalt find him, if thou seek him with all thy heart and with all thy soul.

Be strong and of a good courage, fear not, nor be afraid of them: for the Lord thy God, he it is that doth go with thee; he will not fail thee, nor forsake thee.

Deuteronomy 31:6

This book of the law shall not depart out of thy mouth; but thou shalt meditate therein day and night, that thou mayest observe to do according to all that is written therein: for then thou shalt make thy way prosperous, and then thou shalt have good success.

Have not I commanded thee? Be strong and of a good courage; be not afraid, neither be thou dismayed: for the Lord thy God is with thee whithersoever thou goest.

Joshua 1:8,9

And David said to Solomon his son, Be strong and of good courage, and do it: fear not, nor be dismayed: for the Lord God, even my God, will be with thee; he will not fail thee, nor forsake thee, until thou hast finished all the work for the service of the house of the Lord.

1 Chronicles 28:20

Teach me thy way, O Lord, and lead me in a plain path, because of mine enemies.

Psalm 27:11

For thou art my rock and my fortress; therefore for thy name's sake lead me, and guide me.

Psalm 31:3

For with thee is the fountain of life: in thy light shall we see light.

Psalm 36:9

What time I am afraid, I will trust in thee.

In God I will praise his word, in God I have put my trust; I will not fear what flesh can do unto me.

Psalm 56:3,4

Unto the upright there ariseth light in the darkness: he is gracious, and full of compassion, and righteous.

He shall not be afraid of evil tidings: his heart is fixed, trusting in the Lord.

Psalm 112:4,7

It is better to trust in the Lord than to put confidence in man.

Psalm 118:8

Thy word is a lamp unto my feet, and a light unto my path.

Psalm 119:105

Trust in the Lord with all thine heart; and lean not unto thine own understanding.

Proverbs 3:5

The name of the Lord is a strong tower: the righteous runneth into it, and is safe.

Proverbs 18:10

Nay, in all these things we are more than conquerors through him that loved us.

Romans 8:37

I can do all things through Christ which strengtheneth me.

Philippians 4:13

But there is a spirit in man: and the inspiration of the Almighty giveth them understanding.

Job 32:8

I will bless the Lord, who hath given me counsel: my reins also instruct me in the night seasons.

Psalm 16:7

3

THE BUSINESSWOMAN AND TIME-MANAGEMENT

Overcoming Disorganization

Shew me thy ways, O Lord; teach me thy paths.

Psalm 25:4

I will instruct thee and teach thee in the way which thou shalt go: I will guide thee with mine eye.

Psalm 32:8

Cast thy burden upon the Lord, and he shall sustain thee: he shall never suffer the righteous to be moved.

Psalm 55:22

Trust in the Lord with all thine heart; and lean not unto thine own understanding.

In all thy ways acknowledge him, and he shall direct thy paths.

Proverbs 3:5,6

Ponder the path of thy feet, and let all thy ways be established.

Proverbs 4:26

A man's heart deviseth his way: but the Lord directeth his steps.

Proverbs 16:9

And thine ears shall hear a word behind thee, saying, This is the way, walk ye in it, when ye turn to the right hand, and when ye turn to the left.

Isaiah 30:21

He giveth power to the faint; and to them that have no might he increaseth strength.

Isaiah 40:29

For the Lord God will help me; therefore shall I not be confounded.

Isaiah 50:7a

O Lord, I know that the way of man is not in himself: it is not in man that walketh to direct his steps.

Jeremiah 10:23

And he said unto them, "Come ye yourselves apart into a desert place, and rest a while:" for there were many coming and going, and they had no leisure so much as to eat.

Mark 6:31

For God is not the author of confusion, but of peace, as in all churches of the saints.

1 Corinthians 14:33

Therefore, my beloved brethren, be ye stedfast, unmoveable, always abounding in the work of the Lord, for as much as ye know that your labour is not in vain in the Lord.

1 Corinthians 15:58

And let us not be weary in well doing: for in due season we shall reap, if we faint not.

Galatians 6:9

Be careful for nothing; but in every thing by prayer and supplication with thanksgiving let your requests be made known unto God.

And the peace of God, which passeth all understanding, shall keep your hearts and minds through Christ Jesus.

Philippians 4:6,7

For God hath not given us the spirit of fear; but of power, and of love, and of a sound mind.

2 Timothy 1:7

If any of you lack wisdom, let him ask of God, that giveth to all men liberally, and upbraideth not; and it shall be given him.

James 1:5

Working Through an Overloaded Schedule

The Lord also will be a refuge for the oppressed, a refuge in times of trouble.

Psalm 9:9

Cast thy burden upon the Lord, and he shall sustain thee: he shall never suffer the righteous to be moved.

Psalm 55:22

Unless the Lord had been my help, my soul had almost dwelt in silence.

When I said, My foot slippeth; thy mercy, O Lord, held me up.

Psalm 94:17,18

Great peace have they which love thy law: and nothing shall offend them.

Psalm 119:165

Quicken me, O Lord, for thy name's sake: for thy righteousness' sake bring my soul out of trouble.

Psalm 143:11

When thou liest down, thou shalt not be afraid: yea, thou shalt lie down, and thy sleep shall be sweet.

Proverbs 3:24

But they that wait upon the Lord shall renew their strength; they shall mount up with wings as eagles; they shall run, and not be weary; and they shall walk, and not faint.

Isaiah 40:31

For the Lord God will help me; therefore shall I not be confounded.

Isaiah 50:7a

That he would grant you, according to the riches of his glory, to be strengthened with might by his Spirit in the inner man.

Ephesians 3:16

Be careful for nothing; but in every thing by prayer and supplication with thanksgiving let your requests be made known unto God.

And the peace of God, which passeth all understanding, shall keep your hearts and minds through Christ Jesus.

I can do all things through Christ which strengtheneth me.

Philippians 4:6,7,13

If any of you lack wisdom, let him ask of God, that giveth to all men liberally, and upbraideth not; and it shall be given him.

James 1:5

Cast me not away from thy presence; and take not thy holy spirit from me.

Restore unto me the joy of thy salvation; and uphold me with thy free spirit.

Psalm 51:11,12

And the spirit of the Lord shall rest upon him, the spirit of wisdom and understanding, the spirit of counsel and might, the spirit of knowledge and of the fear of the Lord.

Isaiah 11:2

For I will pour water upon him that is thirsty, and floods upon the dry ground: I will pour my spirit upon thy seed, and my blessing upon thine offspring:

And they shall spring up as among the grass, as willows by the water courses.

Isaiah 44:3,4

But truly I am full of power by the spirit of the Lord, and of judgment, and of might, to declare unto Jacob his transgression, and to Israel his sin.

Micah 3:8

It is the spirit that quickeneth; the flesh profiteth nothing: the words that I speak unto you, they are spirit, and they are life.

John 6:63

Even the Spirit of truth; whom the world cannot receive, because it seeth him not, neither knoweth him: but ye know him; for he dwelleth with you, and shall be in you.

But the Comforter, which is the Holy Ghost, whom the Father will send in my name, he shall teach you all things, and bring all things to your remembrance, whatsoever I have said unto you.

John 14:17,26

Howbeit when he, the Spirit of truth, is come, he will guide you into all truth: for he shall not speak of himself; but whatsoever he shall hear, that shall he speak: and he will shew you things to come.

John 16:13

Likewise the Spirit also helpeth our infirmities: for we know not what we should pray for as we ought: but the Spirit itself maketh intercession for us with groanings which cannot be uttered.

And he that searcheth the hearts knoweth what is the mind of the Spirit, because he maketh intercession for the saints according to the will of God.

Who shall separate us from the love of Christ? shall tribulation, or distress, or persecution, or famine, or nakedness, or peril, or sword?

Nay, in all these things we are more than conquerors through him that loved us.

Romans 8:26,27,35,37

Now the God of hope fill you with all joy and peace in believing, that ye may abound in hope, through the power of the Holy Ghost.

Romans 15:13

Finally, my brethren, be strong in the Lord, and in the power of his might.

Above all, taking the shield of faith, wherewith ye shall be able to quench all the fiery darts of the wicked.

Praying always with all prayer and supplication in the Spirit, and watching thereunto with all perseverance and supplication for all saints.
Ephesians 6:10,16,18

But ye, beloved, building up yourselves on your most holy faith, praying in the Holy Ghost.
Jude 1:20

56

4

THE BUSINESSWOMAN AND HER FAMILY

Helping a Family Member Who Is Sick

And the Lord will take away from thee all sickness, and will put none of the evil diseases of Egypt, which thou knowest, upon thee; but will lay them upon all them that hate thee.

Deuteronomy 7:15

Bless the Lord, O my soul, and forget not all his benefits:

Who forgiveth all thine iniquities; who healeth all thy diseases.

Psalm 103:2,3

My son, attend to my words; incline thine ear unto my sayings.

Let them not depart from thine eyes; keep them in the midst of thine heart.

For they are life unto those that find them, and health to all their flesh.

Proverbs 4:20-22

Surely he hath borne our griefs, and carried our sorrows: yet we did esteem him stricken, smitten of God, and afflicted.

But he was wounded for our transgressions, he was bruised for our iniquities: the chastisement of our peace was upon him; and with his stripes we are healed.

Isaiah 53:4,5

Heal me, O Lord, and I shall be healed; save me, and I shall be saved: for thou art my praise.

Jeremiah 17:14

For I will restore health unto thee, and I will heal thee of thy wounds, saith the Lord.

Jeremiah 30:17a

And Jesus saith unto him, I will come and heal him.

Matthew 8:7

Jesus Christ the same yesterday, and to day, and for ever.

Hebrews 13:8

Is any among you afflicted? let him pray. Is any merry? let him sing psalms.

Is any sick among you? let him call for the elders of the church; and let them pray over him, anointing him with oil in the name of the Lord:

And the prayer of faith shall save the sick, and the Lord shall raise him up; and if he have committed sins, they shall be forgiven him.

Confess your faults one to another, and pray one for another, that ye may be healed. The effectual fervent prayer of a righteous man availeth much.

James 5:13-16

Beloved, I wish above all things that thou mayest prosper and be in health, even as thy soul prospereth.

3 John 2

Dealing With Insufficient Family Time

Only take heed to thyself, and keep thy soul diligently, lest thou forget the things which thine eyes have seen, and lest they depart from thy heart all the days of thy life: but teach them thy sons, and thy sons' sons.

Deuteronomy 4:9

And these words, which I command thee this day, shall be in thine heart:

And thou shalt teach them diligently unto thy children, and shalt talk of them when thou sittest in thine house, and when thou walkest by the way, and when thou liest down, and when thou risest up.

Deuteronomy 6:6,7

Therefore shall ye lay up these my words in your heart and in your soul, and bind them for a sign upon your hand, that they may be as frontlets between your eyes.

And ye shall teach them your children, speaking of them when thou sittest in thine house, and when thou walkest by the way, when thou liest down, and when thou risest up.

Deuteronomy 11:18,19

For he established a testimony in Jacob, and appointed a law in Israel, which he commanded our fathers, that they should make them known to their children.

Psalm 78:5

That the generation to come might know them, even the children which should be born; who should arise and declare them to their children:

That they might set their hope in God, and not forget the works of God, but keep his commandments.

Psalm 78:6,7

So teach us to number our days, that we may apply our hearts unto wisdom.

Psalm 90:12

Blessed is every one that feareth the Lord; that walketh in his ways.

For thou shalt eat the labour of thine hands: happy shalt thou be, and it shall be well with thee.

Thy wife shall be as a fruitful vine by the sides of thine house: thy children like olive plants round about thy table.

Behold, that thus shall the man be blessed that feareth the Lord.

Psalm 128:1-4

A man's heart deviseth his way: but the Lord directeth his steps.

Proverbs 16:9

The just man walketh in his integrity: his children are blessed after him.

Proverbs 20:7

Train up a child in the way he should go: and when he is old, he will not depart from it.

Proverbs 22:6

The father of the righteous shall greatly rejoice: and he that begetteth a wise child shall have joy of him.

Proverbs 23:24

Through wisdom is an house builded; and by understanding it is established.

Proverbs 24:3

Correct thy son, and he shall give thee rest; yea, he shall give delight unto thy soul.

Proverbs 29:17

And wisdom and knowledge shall be the stability of thy times, and strength of salvation: the fear of the Lord is his treasure.

Isaiah 33:6

And all thy children shall be taught of the Lord; and great shall be the peace of thy children.

In righteousness shalt thou be established: thou shalt be far from oppression; for thou shalt not fear: and from terror; for it shall not come near thee.

Isaiah 54:13,14

Tell ye your children of it, and let your children tell their children, and their children another generation.

Joel 1:3

But seek ye first the kingdom of God, and his righteousness; and all these things shall be added unto you.

Matthew 6:33

See then that ye walk circumspectly, not as fools, but as wise,

Redeeming the time, because the days are evil.

Ephesians 5:15,16

And, ye fathers, provoke not your children to wrath: but bring them up in the nurture and admonition of the Lord.

Ephesians 6:4

Walk in wisdom toward them that are without, redeeming the time.

Colossians 4:5

One that ruleth well his own house, having his children in subjection with all gravity;

For if a man know not how to rule his own house, how shall he take care of the church of God?

1 Timothy 3:4,5

But if any provide not for his own, and specially for those of his own house, he hath denied the faith, and is worse than an infidel.

1 Timothy 5:8

Facing Marital Problems

And the Lord God said, It is not good that the man should be alone; I will make him an help meet for him.

Therefore shall a man leave his father and his mother, and shall cleave unto his wife: and they shall be one flesh.

Genesis 2:18,24

Hatred stirreth up strifes: but love covereth all sins.

Proverbs 10:12

To appoint unto them that mourn in Zion, to give unto them beauty for ashes, the oil of joy for mourning, the garment of praise for the spirit of heaviness; that they might be called trees of righteousness, the planting of the Lord, that he might be glorified.

Isaiah 61:3

For if ye forgive men their trespasses, your heavenly Father will also forgive you:

But if ye forgive not men their trespasses, neither will your Father forgive your trespasses.

Matthew 6:14,15

And the Pharisees came to him, and asked him, Is it lawful for a man to put away his wife? tempting him.

And he answered and said unto them, What did Moses command you?

And they said, Moses suffered to write a bill of divorcement, and to put her away.

And Jesus answered and said unto them, For the hardness of your heart he wrote you this precept.

But from the beginning of the creation God made them male and female.

What therefore God hath joined together, let not man put asunder.

Mark 10:2-6,9

Defraud ye not one the other, except it be with consent for a time, that ye may give yourselves to fasting and prayer; and come together again, that Satan tempt you not for your incontinency.

And unto the married I command, yet not I, but the Lord, Let not the wife depart from her husband.

1 Corinthians 7:5,10

Charity suffereth long, and is kind; charity envieth not; charity vaunteth not itself, is not puffed up,

Beareth all things, believeth all things, hopeth all things, endureth all things.

1 Corinthians 13:4,7

Submitting yourselves one to another in the fear of God.

Wives, submit yourselves unto your own husbands, as unto the Lord.

Husbands, love your wives, even as Christ also loved the church, and gave himself for it;

So ought men to love their wives as their own bodies. He that loveth his wife loveth himself.

Nevertheless let every one of you in particular so love his wife even as himself; and the wife see that she reverence her husband.

Ephesians 5:21,22,25,28,33

Wives, submit yourselves unto your own husbands, as it is fit in the Lord.

Husbands, love your wives, and be not bitter against them.

Colossians 3:18,19

5

THE BUSINESS WOMAN AND HER FINANCES

A good man sheweth favour, and lendeth: he will guide his affairs with discretion.

Psalm 112:5

He becometh poor that dealeth with a slack hand: but the hand of the diligent maketh rich.

Proverbs 10:4

The hand of the diligent shall bear rule: but the slothful shall be under tribute.

Proverbs 12:24

The soul of the sluggard desireth, and hath nothing: but the soul of the diligent shall be made fat.

Proverbs 13:4

Love not sleep, lest thou come to poverty; open thine eyes, and thou shalt be satisfied with bread.

Proverbs 20:13

Seest thou a man diligent in his business? he shall stand before kings; he shall not stand before mean men.

Proverbs 22:29

He that tilleth his land shall have plenty of bread: but he that followeth after vain persons shall have poverty enough.

Proverbs 28:19

But seek ye first the kingdom of God, and his righteousness; and all these things shall be added unto you.

Matthew 6:33

Give, and it shall be given unto you; good measure, pressed down, and shaken together, and running over, shall men give into your bosom. For with the same measure that ye mete withal it shall be measured to you again.

Luke 6:38

Not slothful in business; fervent in spirit; serving the Lord.

Romans 12:11

But this I say, He which soweth sparingly shall reap also sparingly; and he which soweth bountifully shall reap also bountifully.

2 Corinthians 9:6

But my God shall supply all your need according to his riches in glory by Christ Jesus.

Philippians 4:19

But thou shalt remember the Lord thy God: for it is he that giveth thee power to get wealth, that he may establish his covenant which he sware unto thy fathers, as it is this day.

Deuteronomy 8:18

Keep therefore the words of this covenant, and do them, that ye may prosper in all that ye do.

Deuteronomy 29:9

Only be thou strong and very courageous, that thou mayest observe to do according to all the law, which Moses my servant commanded thee: turn not from it to the right hand or to the left, that thou mayest prosper whithersoever thou goest.

This book of the law shall not depart out of thy mouth; but thou shalt meditate therein day and night, that thou mayest observe to do according to all that is written therein: for then thou shalt make thy way prosperous, and then thou shalt have good success.

Joshua 1:7,8

I lead in the way of righteousness, in the midst of the paths of judgment:

That I may cause those that love me to inherit substance; and I will fill their treasures.

Proverbs 8:20,21

And the Lord shall guide thee continually, and satisfy thy soul in drought, and make fat thy bones: and thou shalt be like a watered garden, and like a spring of water, whose waters fail not.

Isaiah 58:11

Beloved, I wish above all things that thou mayest prosper and be in health, even as thy soul prospereth.

3 John 2

And let the beauty of the Lord our God be upon us: and establish thou the work of our hands upon us; yea, the work of our hands establish thou it.

Psalm 90:17

A good man sheweth favour, and lendeth: he will guide his affairs with discretion.

Surely he shall not be moved for ever: the righteous shall be in everlasting remembrance.

He shall not be afraid of evil tidings: his heart is fixed, trusting in the Lord.

His heart is established, he shall not be afraid, until he see his desire upon his enemies.

Psalm 112:5-8

Commit thy works unto the Lord, and thy thoughts shall be established.

Proverbs 16:3

Therefore take no thought, saying, What shall we eat? or, What shall we drink? or, Where withal shall we be clothed?

For after all these things do the Gentiles seek: for your heavenly Father knoweth that ye have need of all these things.

But seek ye first the kingdom of God, and his righteousness; and all these things shall be added unto you.

Matthew 6:31-33

Beware that thou forget not the Lord thy God, in not keeping his commandments, and his judgments, and his statutes, which I command thee this day:

But thou shalt remember the Lord thy God: for it is he that giveth thee power to get wealth, that he may establish his covenant which he sware unto thy fathers, as it is this day.

Deuteronomy 8:11,18

He that walketh righteously, and speaketh uprightly; he that despiseth the gain of oppressions, that shaketh his hands from holding of bribes, that stoppeth his ears from hearing of blood, and shutteth his eyes from seeing evil;

He shall dwell on high: his place of defence shall be the munitions of rocks: bread shall be given him; his waters shall be sure.

Isaiah 33:15,16

Let him that stole steal no more: but rather let him labour, working with his hands the thing which is good, that he may have to give to him that needeth.

Ephesians 4:28

Be ye strong therefore, and let not your hands be weak: for your work shall be rewarded.

2 Chronicles 15:7

Vow, and pay unto the Lord your God: let all that be round about him bring presents unto him that ought to be feared.

Psalm 76:11

A good man sheweth favour, and lendeth: he will guide his affairs with discretion.

He hath dispersed, he hath given to the poor; his righteousness endureth for ever; his horn shall be exalted with honour.

Psalm 112:5,9

Honour the Lord with thy substance, and with the firstfruits of all thine increase:

So shall thy barns be filled with plenty, and thy presses shall burst out with new wine.

Proverbs 3:9,10

He becometh poor that dealeth with a slack hand: but the hand of the diligent maketh rich.

Proverbs 10:4

He that hath pity upon the poor lendeth unto the Lord; and that which he hath given will he pay him again.

Proverbs 19:17

He coveteth greedily all the day long: but the righteous giveth and spareth not.

Proverbs 21:26

He that hath a bountiful eye shall be blessed; for he giveth of his bread to the poor.

Proverbs 22:9

He that giveth unto the poor shall not lack: but he that hideth his eyes shall have many a curse.

Proverbs 28:27

Cast thy bread upon the waters: for thou shalt find it after many days.

Ecclesiastes 11:1

If ye be willing and obedient, ye shall eat the good of the land.

Isaiah 1:19

Bring ye all the tithes into the storehouse, that there may be meat in mine house, and prove me now herewith, saith the Lord of hosts, if I will not open you the windows of heaven, and pour you out a blessing, that there shall not be room enough to receive it.

And I will rebuke the devourer for you sakes, and he shall not destroy the fruits of your ground; neither shall your vine cast her fruit before the time in the field, saith the Lord of hosts.

Malachi 3:10,11

Give to him that asketh thee, and from him that would borrow of thee turn not thou away.

Matthew 5:42

Give, and it shall be given unto you; good measure, pressed down, and shaken together, and running over, shall men give into your bosom. For with the same measure that ye mete withal it shall be measured to you again.

Luke 6:38

Upon the first day of the week let every one of you lay by him in store, as God hath prospered him, that there be no gatherings when I come.

I Corinthians 16:2

But this I say, He which soweth sparingly shall reap also sparingly; and he which soweth bountifully shall reap also bountifully.

Every man according as he purposeth in his heart, so let him give; not grudgingly, or of necessity: for God loveth a cheerful giver.

And God is able to make all grace abound toward you; that ye, always having all sufficiency in all things, may abound to every good work.

2 Corinthians 9:6-8

Charge them that are rich in this world, that they be not high minded, nor trust in uncertain riches, but in the living God, who giveth us richly all things to enjoy;

That they do good, that they be rich in good works, ready to distrubute, willing to communicate;

Laying up in store for themselves a good foundation against the time to come, that they may lay hold on eternal life.

I Timothy 6:17-19

But whoso hath this world's good, and seeth his brother have need, and shutteth up his bowels of compassion from him, how dwelleth the love of God in him?

My little children let us not love in word, niether in tongue; but in deed and in truth.

1 John 3:17,18

6
THE BUSINESS WOMAN AND HER PERSONAL LIFE

Dealing With Stress

One man of you shall chase a thousand: for the Lord your God, he it is that fighteth for you, as he hath promised you.

Joshua 23:10

He will keep the feet of his saints, and the wicked shall be silent in darkness; for by strength shall no man prevail.

1 Samuel 2:9

Thus saith the Lord unto you, Be not afraid nor dismayed by reason of this great multitude; for the battle is not yours, but God's.

2 Chronicles 20:15b

But thou, O Lord, art a shield for me; my glory, and the lifter up of mine head.

Psalm 3:3

My voice shalt thou hear in the morning, O Lord; in the morning will I direct my prayer unto thee, and will look up.

Psalm 5:3

The Lord also will be a refuge for the oppressed, a refuge in times of trouble.

Psalm 9:9

I will love thee, O Lord, my strength.
The Lord is my rock, and my fortress, and my deliverer; my God, my strength, in whom I will trust; my buckler, and the horn of my salvation, and my high tower.

Psalm 18:1,2

Though an host should encamp against me, my heart shall not fear: though war should rise against me, in this will I be confident.
For in the time of trouble he shall hide me in his pavilion: in the secret of his tabernacle shall he hide me; he shall set me up upon a rock.

Psalm 27:3,5

My flesh and my heart faileth: but God is the strength of my heart, and my portion for ever.

Psalm 73:26

Bless the Lord, O my soul, and forget not all his benefits:
Who satisfieth thy mouth with good things; so that thy youth is renewed like the eagle's.

Psalm 103:2,5

He sent his word, and healed them, and delivered them from their destructions.

Psalm 107:20

Peace be within thy walls, and prosperity within thy palaces.

Psalm 122:7

It is vain for you to rise up early, to sit up late, to eat the bread of sorrows: for so he giveth his beloved sleep.

Psalm 127:2

When thou liest down, thou shalt not be afraid: yea, thou shalt lie down, and thy sleep shall be sweet.

Proverbs 3:24

The wicked are overthrown, and are not: but the house of the righteous shall stand.

Proverbs 12:7

In the fear of the Lord is strong confidence: and his children shall have a place of refuge.

Proverbs 14:26

He giveth power to the faint; and to them that have no might he increaseth strength.

But they that wait upon the Lord shall renew their strength; they shall mount up with wings as eagles; they shall run, and not be weary; and they shall walk, and not faint.

Isaiah 40:29,31

Fear thou not; for I am with thee: be not dismayed; for I am thy God: I will strengthen thee; yea, I will help thee; yea, I will uphold thee with the right hand of my righteousness.

Isaiah 41:10

Not by might, nor by power, but by my spirit, saith the Lord of hosts.

Zechariah 4:6b

Let not your heart be troubled: ye believe in God, believe also in me.

Peace I leave with you, my peace I give unto you: not as the world giveth, give I unto you. Let not your heart be troubled, neither let it be afraid.

John 14:1,27

Be careful for nothing; but in every thing by prayer and supplication with thanksgiving let your requests be made known unto God.

And the peace of God, which passeth all understanding, shall keep your hearts and minds through Christ Jesus.

Philippians 4:6,7

Casting all your care upon him; for he careth for you.

1 Peter 5:7

The Lord knoweth how to deliver the godly out of temptations, and to reserve the unjust unto the day of judgment to be punished.

2 Peter 2:9

Dealing with Being Overworked

I will both lay me down in peace, and sleep: for thou, Lord, only makest me dwell in safety.
Psalm 4:8

He maketh me to lie down in green pastures: he leadeth me beside the still waters.

He restoreth my soul: he leadeth me in the paths of righteousness for his name's sake.
Psalm 23:2,3

The Lord will give strength unto his people; the Lord will bless his people with peace.
Psalm 29:11

Delight thyself also in the Lord; and he shall give thee the desires of thine heart.

Commit thy way unto the Lord; trust also in him; and he shall bring it to pass.

Rest in the Lord, and wait patiently for him: fret not thyself because of him who prospereth in his way, because of the man who bringeth wicked devices to pass.

But the meek shall inherit the earth; and shall delight themselves in the abundance of peace.
Psalm 37:4,5,7,11

My flesh and my heart faileth: but God is the strength of my heart, and my portion for ever.
Psalm 73:26

I will hear what God the Lord will speak: for he will speak peace unto his people, and to his saints: but let them not turn again to folly.
Psalm 85:8

Thou wilt keep him in perfect peace, whose mind is stayed on thee: because he trusteth in thee.

Isaiah 26:3

To whom he said, This is the rest wherewith ye may cause the weary to rest; and this is the refreshing: yet they would not hear.

Isaiah 28:12

For thus saith the Lord God, the Holy One of Israel; In returning and rest shall ye be saved; in quietness and in confidence shall be your strength: and ye would not.

Isaiah 30:15

Come unto me, all ye that labour and are heavy laden, and I will give you rest.

Take my yoke upon you, and learn of me; for I am meek and lowly in heart: and ye shall find rest unto your souls.

Matthew 11:28,29

And he said unto them, Come ye yourselves apart into a desert place, and rest a while: for there were many coming and going, and they had no leisure so much as to eat.

Mark 6:31

Peace I leave with you, my peace I give unto you: not as the world giveth, give I unto you. Let not your heart be troubled, neither let it be afraid.

John 14:27

Facing Controversy

My lips shall not speak wickedness, nor my tongue utter deceit.

Job 27:4

For thou art my rock and my fortress; therefore for thy name's sake lead me, and guide me.

Pull me out of the net that they have laid privily for me: for thou art my strength.

Into thine hand I commit my spirit: thou hast redeemed me, O Lord God of truth.

Psalm 31:3-5

Thou art my hiding place; thou shalt preserve me from trouble; thou shalt compass me about with songs of deliverance.

Psalm 32:7

Commit thy way unto the Lord; trust also in him; and he shall bring it to pass.

And he shall bring forth thy righteousness as the light, and thy judgment as the noon day.

Rest in the Lord, and wait patiently for him: fret not thyself because of him who prospereth in his way, because of the man who bringeth wicked devices to pass.

Psalm 37:5-7

For in thee, O Lord, do I hope: thou wilt hear, O Lord my God.

Psalm 38:15

Whoso offereth praise glorifieth me: and to him that ordereth his conversation aright will I shew the salvation of God.

Psalm 50:23

In my distress I cried unto the Lord, and he heard me.

Deliver my soul, O Lord, from lying lips, and from a deceitful tongue.

Psalm 120:1,2

Though I walk in the midst of trouble, thou wilt revive me: thou shalt stretch forth thine hand against the wrath of mine enemies, and thy right hand shall save me.

Psalm 138:7

These six things doth the Lord hate: yea, seven are an abomination unto him:

A proud look, a lying tongue, and hands that shed innocent blood,

An heart that deviseth wicked imaginations, feet that be swift in running to mischief,

A false witness that speaketh lies, and he that soweth discord among brethren.

Proverbs 6:16-19

The lip of truth shall be established forever: but a lying tongue is but for a moment.

Proverbs 12:19

Say not, I will do so to him as he hath done to me: I will render to the man according to his work.

Proverbs 24:29

When thou passest through the waters, I will be with thee; and through the rivers, they shall not overflow thee: when thou walkest through the fire, thou shalt not be burned; neither shall the flame kindle upon thee.

Isaiah 43:2

And the Lord shall guide thee continually, and satisfy thy soul in drought, and make fat thy bones: and thou shalt be like a watered garden, and like a spring of water, whose waters fail not.

Isaiah 58:11

The Lord is good, a strong hold in the day of trouble; and he knoweth them that trust in him.

Nahum 1:7

And when ye stand praying, forgive, if ye have ought against any: that your Father also which is in heaven may forgive you your trespasses.

But if ye do not forgive, neither will your Father which is in heaven forgive your trespasses.

Mark 11:25,26

And who is he that will harm you, if ye be followers of that which is good?

1 Peter 3:13

Casting all your care upon him; for he careth for you.

1 Peter 5:7

Dealing With Feeling Threatened

After these things the word of the Lord came unto Abram in a vision, saying, Fear not, Abram: I am thy shield, and thy exceeding great reward.

Genesis 15:1

Happy art thou, O Israel: who is like unto thee, O people saved by the Lord, the shield of thy help, and who is the sword of thy excellency! and thine enemies shall be found liars unto thee; and thou shalt tread upon their high places.

Deuteronomy 33:29

And he said, The Lord is my rock, and my fortress, and my deliverer.

Samuel 22:2

Lord, how are they increased that trouble me! many are they that rise up against me.

Many there be which say of my soul, There is no help for him in God.

But thou, O Lord, art a shield for me; my glory, and the lifter up of mine head.

Psalm 3:1-3

In my distress I called upon the Lord, and cried unto my God: he heard my voice out of his temple, and my cry came before him, even into his ears.

Thou hast also given me the shield of thy salvation: and thy right hand hath holden me up, and thy gentleness hath made me great.

Psalm 18:6,35

The Lord is my strength and my shield; my heart trusted in him, and I am helped: therefore my heart greatly rejoiceth; and with my song will I praise him.

Psalm 28:7

The angel of the Lord encampeth round about them that fear him, and delivereth them.

Psalm 34:7

What time I am afraid, I will trust in thee.

In God I will praise his word, in God I have put my trust; I will not fear what flesh can do unto me.

Psalm 56:3,4

For the Lord God is a sun and shield: the Lord will give grace and glory: no good thing will he withhold from them that walk uprightly.

Psalm 84:11

He shall cover thee with his feathers, and under his wings shalt thou trust: his truth shall be thy shield and buckler.

Psalm 91:4

Ye that fear the Lord, trust in the Lord: he is their help and their shield.

Psalm 115:11

Thou art my hiding place and my shield: I hope in thy word.

Psalm 119:114

My goodness, and my fortress; my high tower, and my deliverer; my shield, and he in whom I trust; who subdueth my people under me.

Psalm 144:2

Fear thou not; for I am with thee: be not dismayed; for I am thy God: I will strengthen thee; yea, I will help thee; yea, I will uphold thee with the right hand of my righteousness.

For I the Lord thy God will hold thy right hand, saying unto thee, Fear not; I will help thee.

Isaiah 41:10,13

Above all, taking the shield of faith, wherewith ye shall be able to quench all the fiery darts of the wicked.

Ephesians 6:16

Dealing with Depression

For his anger endureth but a moment; in his favour is life: weeping may endure for a night, but joy cometh in the morning.

Psalm 30:5

Behold, the eye of the Lord is upon them that fear him, upon them that hope in his mercy.
Psalm 33:18

The righteous cry, and the Lord heareth, and delivereth them out of all their troubles.
Psalm 34:17

When I remember thee upon my bed, and meditate on thee in the night watches.
Psalm 63:6

I will praise thee with my whole heart: before the gods will I sing praise unto thee.
Psalm 138:1

He healeth the broken in heart, and bindeth up their wounds.
Psalm 147:3

Happy is the man that findeth wisdom, and the man that getteth understanding.

Her ways are ways of pleasantness, and all her paths are peace.

She is a tree of life to them that lay hold upon her: and happy is every one that retaineth her.
Proverbs 3:13,17,18

The wilderness and the solitary place shall be glad for them; and the desert shall rejoice, and blossom as the rose.

And the ransomed of the Lord shall return, and come to Zion with songs and everlasting joy upon their heads: they shall obtain joy and gladness, and sorrow and sighing shall flee away.

Isaiah 35:1,10

But they that wait upon the Lord shall renew their strength; they shall mount up with wings as eagles; they shall run, and not be weary; and they shall walk, and not faint.

Isaiah 40:31

Fear thou not; for I am with thee: be not dismayed; for I am thy God: I will strengthen thee; yea, I will help thee; yea, I will uphold thee with the right hand of my righteousness.

Isaiah 41:10

When thou passest through the waters, I will be with thee; and through the rivers, they shall not overflow thee: when thou walkest through the fire, thou shalt not be burned; neither shall the flame kindle upon thee.

Isaiah 43:2

To appoint unto them that mourn in Zion, to give unto them beauty for ashes, the oil of joy for mourning, the garment of praise for the spirit of heaviness; that they might be called trees of righteousness, the planting of the Lord, that he might be glorified.

Isaiah 61:3

For I am persuaded, that neither death, nor life, nor angels, nor principalities, nor powers, nor things present, nor things to come,

Nor height, nor depth, nor any other creature, shall be able to separate us from the love of God, which is in Christ Jesus our Lord.

Romans 8:38,39

Blessed be God, even the Father of our Lord Jesus Christ, the Father of mercies, and the God of all comfort;

Who comforteth us in all our tribulation, that we may be able to comfort them which are in any trouble, by the comfort wherewith we ourselves are comforted of God.

2 Corinthians 1:3,4

Beloved, think it not strange concerning the fiery trial which is to try you, as though some strange thing happened unto you:

But rejoice, inasmuch as ye are partakers of Christ's sufferings; that, when his glory shall be revealed, ye may be glad also with exceeding joy.

1 Peter 4:12,13

91

Overcoming Feeling Lonely

The eternal God is thy refuge, and underneath are the everlasting arms: and he shall thrust out the enemy from before thee; and shall say, Destroy them.

Deuteronomy 33:27

For the Lord will not forsake his people for his great name's sake: because it hath pleased the Lord to make you his people.

1 Samuel 12:22

And they that know thy name will put their trust in thee: for thou, Lord, hast not forsaken them that seek thee.

Psalm 9:10

Yea, though I walk through the valley of the shadow of death, I will fear no evil: for thou art with me; thy rod and thy staff they comfort me.

Psalm 23:4

When my father and my mother forsake me, then the Lord will take me up.

Psalm 27:10

I have been young, and now am old; yet have I not seen the righteous forsaken, nor his seed begging bread.

For the Lord loveth judgment, and forsaketh not his saints; they are preserved for ever: but the seed of the wicked shall be cut off.

Psalm 37:25,28

God is our refuge and strength, a very present help in trouble.

Psalm 46:1

He healeth the broken in heart, and bindeth up their wounds.

Psalm 147:3

For thou hast been a strength to the poor, a strength to the needy in his distress, a refuge from the storm, a shadow from the heat, when the blast of the terrible ones is as a storm against the wall.

Isaiah 25:4

He giveth power to the faint; and to them that have no might he increaseth strength.

Isaiah 40:29

Fear thou not; for I am with thee: be not dismayed; for I am thy God: I will strengthen thee; yea, I will help thee; yea, I will uphold thee with the right hand of my righteousness.

Isaiah 41:10

For the mountains shall depart, and the hills be removed; but my kindness shall not depart from thee, neither shall the covenant of my peace be removed, saith the Lord that hath mercy on thee.

Isaiah 54:10

But the very hairs of your head are all numbered.

Matthew 10:30

Teaching them to observe all things whatsoever I have commanded you: and, lo, I am with you alway, even unto the end of the world. Amen.

Matthew 28:20

Let not your heart be troubled: ye believe in God, believe also in me.

And I will pray the Father, and he shall give you another Comforter, that he may abide with you for ever;

Even the Spirit of truth; whom the world cannot receive, because it seeth him not, neither knoweth him: but ye know him; for he dwelleth with you, and shall be in you.

I will not leave you comfortless: I will come to you.

John 14:1,16-18

And the Lord shall deliver me from every evil work, and will preserve me unto his heavenly kingdom: to whom be glory for ever and ever.

2 Timothy 4:18

For we have not an high priest which cannot be touched with the feeling of our infirmities; but was in all points tempted like as we are, yet without sin.

Let us therefore come boldly unto the throne of grace, that we may obtain mercy, and find grace to help in time of need.

Hebrews 4:15,16

Let your conversation be without covetousness and be content with such things as ye have: for he hath said, I will never leave thee, nor forsake thee.

Hebrews 13:5

Casting all your care upon him; for he careth for you.

1 Peter 5:7

Avoiding the Temptation to Quit

Be strong and of a good courage: for unto this people shalt thou divide for an inheritance the land, which I sware unto their fathers to give them.

Joshua 1:6

And the people the men of Israel encouraged themselves, and set their battle again in array in the place where they put themselves in array the first day.

Judges 20:22

And David was greatly distressed; for the people spake of stoning him, because the soul of all the people was grieved, every man for his sons and for his daughters: but David encouraged himself in the Lord his God.

1 Samuel 30:6

Wait on the Lord: be of good courage, and he shall strengthen thine heart: wait, I say, on the Lord.

Psalm 27:14

Be of good courage, and he shall strengthen your heart, all ye that hope in the Lord.

Psalm 31:24

For in thee, O Lord, do I hope: thou wilt hear, O Lord my God.

Psalm 38:15

And now, Lord, what wait I for? my hope is in thee.

Psalm 39:7

Through thee will we push down our enemies: through thy name will we tread them under that rise up against us.

Psalm 44:5

But I will hope continually, and will yet praise thee more and more.

Psalm 71:14

Happy is he that hath the God of Jacob for his help, whose hope is in the Lord his God.
Psalm 146:5

Know ye that the Lord he is God: it is he that hath made us, and not we ourselves; we are his people, and the sheep of his pasture.
Psalm 100:3

Unto thee lift I up mine eyes, O thou that dwellest in the heavens.

Behold, as the eyes of servants look unto the hand of their masters, and as the eyes of a maiden unto the hand of her mistress; so our eyes wait upon the Lord our God, until that he have mercy upon us.
Psalm 123:1,2

Trust in the Lord with all thine heart; and lean not unto thine own understanding.
Proverbs 3:5

Jesus said unto him, If thou canst believe, all things are possible to him that believeth.

And straightway the father of the child cried out, and said with tears, Lord, I believe; help thou mine unbelief.
Mark 9:23,24

Therefore I say unto you, What things so ever ye desire, when ye pray, believe that ye receive them, and ye shall have them.
Mark 11:24

But if we hope for that we see not, then do we with patience wait for it.

Who shall separate us from the love of Christ? shall tribulation, or distress, or persecution, or famine, or nakedness, or peril, or sword?

As it is written, For thy sake we are killed all the day long; we are accounted as sheep for the slaughter.

Nay, in all these things we are more than conquerors through him that loved us.

For I am persuaded, that neither death, nor life, nor angels, nor principalities, nor powers, nor things present, nor things to come,

Nor height, nor depth, nor any other creature, shall be able to separate us from the love of God, which is in Christ Jesus our Lord.

Romans 8:25,35,36-39

I can do all things through Christ which strengtheneth me.

Philippians 4:13

Strengthened with all might, according to his glorious power, unto all patience and longsuffering with joyfulness.

Colossians 1:11

Now faith is the substance of things hoped for, the evidence of things not seen.

Hebrews 11:1

Ye are of God, little children, and have overcome them: because greater is he that is in you, than he that is in the world.

1 John 4:4

Finding Encouragement

In the day when I cried thou answeredst me, and strengthenedst me with strength in my soul.

Psalm 138:3

Though I walk in the midst of trouble, thou wilt revive me: thou shalt stretch forth thine hand against the wrath of mine enemies, and thy right hand shall save me.

The Lord will perfect that which concerneth me: thy mercy, O Lord, endureth for ever: forsake not the works of thine own hands.

Psalm 138:7,8

But thou, O Lord, be merciful unto me, and raise me up, that I may requite them.

Psalm 41:10

When thou passest through the waters, I will be with thee; and through the rivers, they shall not overflow thee: when thou walkest through the fire, thou shalt not be burned; neither shall the flame kindle upon thee.

Isaiah 43:2

For the Lord shall comfort Zion: he will comfort all her waste places; and he will make her wilderness like Eden, and her desert like the garden of the Lord; joy and gladness shall be found therein, thanksgiving, and the voice of melody.

Isaiah 51:3

I, even I, am he that comforteth you: who art thou, that thou shouldest be afraid of a man that shall die, and of the son of man which shall be made as grass.

Isaiah 51:12

The Lord will perfect that which concerneth me: thy mercy, O Lord, endureth for ever: forsake not the works of thine own hands.

Psalm 138:8

For I know the thoughts that I think toward you, saith the Lord, thoughts of peace, and not of evil, to give you an expected end.

Jeremiah 29:11

Now our Lord Jesus Christ himself, and God, even our Father, which hath loved us, and hath given us everlasting consolation and good hope through grace,

Comfort your hearts, and stablish you in every good word and work.

2 Thessalonians 2:16,17

For God is not unrighteous to forget your work and labour of love, which ye have shewed toward his name, in that ye have ministered to the saints, and do minister.

And we desire that every one of you do shew the same diligence to the full assurance of hope unto the end:

That ye be not slothful, but followers of them who through faith and patience inherit the promises.

Hebrews 6:10-12

But the mercy of the Lord is from everlasting to everlasting upon them that fear him, and his righteousness unto children's children.

Psalm 103:17

Be strong and of a good courage, fear not, nor be afraid of them: for the Lord thy God, he it is that doth go with thee; he will not fail thee, nor forsake thee.

Deuteronomy 31:6

Nevertheless I am continually with thee: thou hast holden me by my right hand.

Psalm 73:23

Have not I commanded thee? Be strong and of a good courage; be not afraid, neither be thou dismayed: for the Lord thy God is with thee whithersoever thou goest.

Joshua 1:9

Then he answered and spake unto me, saying, This is the word of the Lord unto Zerubbabel, saying, Not by might, nor by power, but by my spirit, saith the Lord of hosts.

Zechariah 4:6

Trust in the Lord, and do good; so shalt thou dwell in the land, and verily thou shalt be fed.

Delight thyself also in the Lord; and he shall give thee the desires of thine heart.

Commit thy way unto the Lord; trust also in him; and he shall bring it to pass.

Psalm 37:3-5

O bless our God, ye people, and make the voice of his praise to be heard:

Which holdeth our soul in life, and suffereth not our feet to be moved.

Psalm 66:8,9

Now thanks be unto God, which always causeth us to triumph in Christ, and maketh manifest the savour of his knowledge by us in every place.

2 Corinthians 2:14

I will praise the name of God with a song, and will magnify him with thanksgiving.

Psalm 69:30

The humble shall see this, and be glad: and your heart shall live that seek God.

Psalm 69:32

Being confident of this very thing, that he which hath begun a good work in you will perform it until the day of Jesus Christ.

Philippians 1:6

But the path of the just is as the shining light, that shineth more and more unto the perfect day.

Proverbs 4:18

Facing The Need To Forgive

The discretion of a man deferreth his anger and it is his glory to pass over a transgression.

Proverbs 19:11

Rejoice not when thine enemy falleth, and let not thine heart be glad when he stumbleth:

Say not, I will do so to him as he hath done to me: I will render to the man according to his work.

Proverbs 24:17,29

If thine enemy be hungry, give him bread to eat; and if he be thirsty, give him water to drink.

Proverbs 25:21

Blessed are the merciful: for they shall obtain mercy.

Matthew 5:7

But I say unto you, That ye resist not evil: but whosoever shall smite thee on thy right cheek, turn to him the other also.

Matthew 5:39

But I say unto you, Love your enemies, bless them that curse you, do good to them that hate you, and pray for them which despitefully use you, and persecute you.

Matthew 5:44

And forgive us our debts, as we forgive our debtors.

For if ye forgive men their trespasses, your heavenly Father will also forgive you:

But if ye forgive not men their trespasses, neither will your Father forgive your trespasses.

Matthew 6:12,14-15

Then came Peter to him, and said, Lord, how oft shall my brother sin against me, and I forgive him? till seven times?

Matthew 18:21

Jesus saith unto him, I say not unto thee, Until seven times: but, Until seventy times seven.

Matthew 18:22

And when ye stand praying, forgive, if ye have ought against any: that your Father also which is in heaven may forgive you your trespasses.

Mark 11:25

Take heed to yourselves: If thy brother trespass against thee, rebuke him; and if he repent, forgive him.

And if he trespass against thee seven times in a day, and seven times in a day turn again to thee, saying, I repent; thou shalt forgive him.

Luke 17:3,4

Bless them which persecute you: bless, and curse not.

Be not overcome of evil, but overcome evil with good.

Romans 12:14,21

And be ye kind one to another, tenderhearted, forgiving one another, even as God for Christ's sake hath forgiven you.

Ephesians 4:32

Forbearing one another, and forgiving one another, if any man have a quarrel against any: even as Christ forgave you, so also do ye.

Colossians 3:13

Not rendering evil for evil, or railing for railing: but contrariwise blessing; knowing that ye are thereunto called, that ye should inherit a blessing.

Peter 3:9

Finding Comfort

And I will pray the Father, and he shall give you another Comforter, that he may abide with you for ever;

Even the Spirit of truth; whom the world cannot receive, because it seeth him not, neither knoweth him: but ye know him; for he dwelleth with you, and shall be in you.

I will not leave you comfortless: I will come to you.

John 14:16-18

But the Comforter, which is the Holy Ghost, whom the Father will send in my name, he shall teach you all things, and bring all things to your remembrance, whatsoever I have said unto you.

John 14:26

Nevertheless I tell you the truth; It is expedient for you that I go away: for if I go not away, the Comforter will not come unto you; but if I depart, I will send him unto you.

John 16:7

Blessed be God, even the Father of our Lord Jesus Christ, the Father of mercies, and the God of all comfort;

Who comforteth us in all our tribulation, that we may be able to comfort them which are in any trouble, by the comfort wherewith we ourselves are comforted of God.

For as the sufferings of Christ abound in us, so our consolation also aboundeth by Christ.

2 Corinthians 1:3-5

For he that speaketh in an unknown tongue speaketh not unto men, but unto God: for no man understandeth him; howbeit in the spirit he speaketh mysteries.

But he that prophesieth speaketh unto men to edification, and exhortation, and comfort.

1 Corinthians 14:2,3

Wherefore comfort yourselves together, and edify one another, even as also ye do.

1 Thessalonians 5:11

But ye, beloved, building up yourselves on your most holy faith, praying in the Holy Ghost.
Jude 1:20

And David was greatly distressed; for the people spake of stoning him, because the soul of all the people was grieved, every man for his sons and for his daughters: but David encouraged himself in the Lord his God.
1 Samuel 30:6

The eternal God is thy refuge, and underneath are the everlasting arms: and he shall thrust out the enemy from before thee; and shall say, Destroy them.
Deuteronomy 33:27

Yea, though I walk through the valley of the shadow of death, I will fear no evil: for thou art with me; thy rod and thy staff they comfort me.
Psalm 23:4

For in the time of trouble he shall hide me in his pavilion: in the secret of his tabernacle shall he hide me; he shall set me up upon a rock.
And now shall mine head be lifted up above mine enemies round about me: therefore will I offer in his tabernacle sacrifices of joy; I will sing, yea, I will sing praises unto the Lord.
Psalm 27:5,6

For his anger endureth but a moment; in his favour is life: weeping may endure for a night, but joy cometh in the morning.

Psalm 30:5

I will be glad and rejoice in thy mercy: for thou hast considered my trouble; thou hast known my soul in adversities.

Psalm 31:7

Cast thy burden upon the Lord, and he shall sustain thee: he shall never suffer the righteous to be moved.

Psalm 55:22

Thou tellest my wanderings: put thou my tears into thy bottle: are they not in thy book?

When I cry unto thee, then shall mine enemies turn back: this I know; for God is for me.

In God will I praise his word: in the Lord will I praise his word.

Psalm 56:8-10

This is my comfort in my affliction: for thy word hath quickened me.

Psalm 119:50

I remembered thy judgments of old, O Lord; and have comforted myself.

Psalm 119:52

Thy statutes have been my songs in the house of my pilgrimage.

Psalm 119:54

Finding Faith When You Need It

But what saith it? The word is nigh thee, even in thy mouth, and in thy heart: that is, the word of faith, which we preach.

Romans 10:8

So then faith cometh by hearing, and hearing by the word of God.

Romans 10:17

As for God, his way is perfect; the word of the Lord is tried: he is a buckler to all them that trust in him.

2 Samuel 22:31

The Lord also will be a refuge for the oppressed, a refuge in times of trouble.

And they that know thy name will put their trust in thee: for thou, Lord, hast not forsaken them that seek thee.

Psalm 9:9,10

It is better to trust in the Lord than to put confidence in man.

It is better to trust in the Lord than to put confidence in princes.

Psalm 118:8,9

They that trust in the Lord shall be as mount Zion, which cannot be removed, but abideth for ever.

Psalm 125:1

My help cometh from the Lord, which made heaven and earth.

He will not suffer thy foot to be moved: he that keepeth thee will not slumber.

Behold, he that keepeth Israel shall neither slumber nor sleep.

Psalm 121:2-4

But let all those that put their trust in thee rejoice: let them ever shout for joy, because thou defendest them: let them also that love thy name be joyful in thee.

Psalm 5:11

Now the God of hope fill you with all joy and peace in believing, that ye may abound in hope, through the power of the Holy Ghost.

Romans 15:13

For this cause also thank we God without ceasing, because, when ye received the word of God which ye heard of us, ye received it not as the word of men, but as it is in truth, the word of God, which effectually worketh also in you that believe.

1 Thessalonians 2:13

Now the just shall live by faith: but if any man draw back, my soul shall have no pleasure in him.

But we are not of them who draw back unto perdition; but of them that believe to the saving of the soul.

Hebrews 10:38,39

For whatsoever is born of God overcometh the world: and this is the victory that overcometh the world, even our faith.

1 John 5:4

And the Lord, he it is that doth go before thee; he will be with thee, he will not fail thee, neither forsake thee: fear not, neither be dismayed.

Deuteronomy 31:8

And they rose early in the morning, and went forth into the wilderness of Tekoa: and as they went forth, Jehoshaphat stood and said, Hear me, O Judah, and ye inhabitants of Jerusalem; Believe in the Lord your God, so shall ye be established; believe his prophets, so shall ye prosper.

2 Chronicles 20:20

Be strong and courageous, be not afraid nor dismayed for the king of Assyria, nor for all the multitude that is with him: for there be more with us than with him:

With him is an arm of flesh; but with us is the Lord our God to help us, and to fight our battles. And the people rested themselves upon the words of Hezekiah king of Judah.

2 Chronicles 32:7,8

Fear not, O land; be glad and rejoice: for the Lord will do great things.

Joel 2:21

Behold, his soul which is lifted up is not upright in him: but the just shall live by his faith.

Habakkuk 2:4

And David said to Solomon his son, Be strong and of good courage, and do it: fear not, nor be dismayed: for the Lord God, even my God, will be with thee; he will not fail thee, nor forsake thee, until thou hast finished all the work for the service of the house of the Lord.

1 Chronicles 28:20

The Lord is my shepherd; I shall not want.

Psalm 23:1

Finding Joy

Thou wilt shew me the path of life: in thy presence is fulness of joy; at thy right hand there are pleasures for evermore.

Psalm 16:11

Glory and honour are in his presence; strength and gladness are in his place.

1 Chronicles 16:27

Also that day they offered great sacrifices, and rejoiced: for God had made them rejoice with great joy: the wives also and the children rejoiced: so that the joy of Jerusalem was heard even afar off.

Nehemiah 12:43

Thou hast put gladness in my heart, more than in the time that their corn and their wine increased.

Psalm 4:7

I will be glad and rejoice in thee: I will sing praise to thy name, O thou most High.

Psalm 9:2

The statutes of the Lord are right, rejoicing the heart: the commandment of the Lord is pure, enlightening the eyes.

Psalm 19:8

The Lord is my strength and my shield; my heart trusted in him, and I am helped: therefore my heart greatly rejoiceth; and with my song will I praise him.

Psalm 28:7

And my soul shall be joyful in the Lord: it shall rejoice in his salvation.

Psalm 35:9

Wilt thou not revive us again: that thy people may rejoice in thee?

Psalm 85:6

Blessed is the people that know the joyful sound: they shall walk, O Lord, in the light of thy countenance.

In thy name shall they rejoice all the day: and in thy righteousness shall they be exalted.

Psalm 89:15,16

Make a joyful noise unto the Lord, all ye lands.

Serve the Lord with gladness: come before his presence with singing.

Psalm 100:1,2

When the Lord turned again the captivity of Zion, we were like them that dream.

Then was our mouth filled with laughter, and our tongue with singing: then said they among the heathen, The Lord hath done great things for them.

Psalm 126:1,2

Thy words were found, and I did eat them; and thy word was unto me the joy and rejoicing of mine heart: for I am called by thy name, O Lord God of hosts.

Jeremiah 15:16

Notwithstanding in this rejoice not, that the spirits are subject unto you; but rather rejoice, because your names are written in heaven.

Luke 10:20

These things have I spoken unto you, that my joy might remain in you, and that your joy might be full.

John 15:11

Thou hast made known to me the ways of life; thou shalt make me full of joy with thy countenance.

Acts 2:28

And the disciples were filled with joy, and with the Holy Ghost.

Acts 13:52

For the kingdom of God is not meat and drink; but righteousness, and peace, and joy in the Holy Ghost.

Romans 14:17

For ye were sometimes darkness, but now are ye light in the Lord: walk as children of light.

Ephesians 5:8

Those things, which ye have both learned, and received, and heard, and seen in me, do: and the God of peace shall be with you.

Philippians 4:9

Whom having not seen, ye love; in whom, though now ye see him not, yet believing, ye rejoice with joy unspeakable and full of glory.

1 Peter 1:8

Finding Love When You Really Need It

And hope maketh not ashamed; because the love of God is shed abroad in our hearts by the Holy Ghost which is given unto us.

Romans 5:5

And this I pray, that your love may abound yet more and more in knowledge and in all judgment;

That ye may approve things that are excellent; that ye may be sincere and without offence till the day of Christ;

Being filled with the fruits of righteousness, which are by Jesus Christ, unto the glory and praise of God.

Philippians 1:9-11

And the Lord make you to increase and abound in love one toward another, and toward all men, even as we do toward you:

To the end he may stablish your hearts unblameable in holiness before God, even our Father, at the coming of our Lord Jesus Christ with all his saints.

1 Thessalonians 3:12,13

But as touching brotherly love ye need not that I write unto you: for ye yourselves are taught of God to love one another.

And indeed ye do it toward all the brethren which are in all Macedonia: but we beseech you, brethren, that ye increase more and more.

1 Thessalonians 4:9,10

And the Lord direct your hearts into the love of God, and into the patient waiting for Christ.

2 Thessalonians 3:5

Herein is love, not that we loved God, but that he loved us, and sent his Son to be the propitiation for our sins.

Beloved, if God so loved us, we ought also to love one another.

No man hath seen God at any time. If we love one another, God dwelleth in us, and his love is perfected in us.

1 John 4:10-12

And we have known and believed the love that God hath to us. God is love; and he that dwelleth in love dwelleth in God, and God in him.

Herein is our love made perfect, that we may have boldness in the day of judgment: because as he is, so are we in this world.

There is no fear in love; but perfect love casteth out fear: because fear hath torment. He that feareth is not made perfect in love.

1 John 4:16-18

Hatred stirreth up strifes: but love covereth all sins.

Proverbs 10:12

Set me as a seal upon thine heart, as a seal upon thine arm: for love is strong as death; jealousy is cruel as the grave: the coals thereof are coals of fire, which hath a most vehement flame.

Many waters cannot quench love, neither can the floods drown it: if a man would give all the substance of his house for love, it would utterly be contemned.

Song of Solomon 8:6,7

A friend loveth at all times, and a brother is born for adversity.

Proverbs 17:17

Honour thy father and thy mother: and, Thou shalt love thy neighbour as thyself.

Matthew 19:19

And thou shalt love the Lord thy God with all thine heart, and with all thy soul, and with all thy might.

Deuteronomy 6:5

And now, Israel, what doth the Lord thy God require of thee, but to fear the Lord thy God, to walk in all his ways, and to love him, and to serve the Lord thy God with all thy heart and with all thy soul.

Deuteronomy 10:12

But take diligent heed to do the commandment and the law, which Moses the servant of the Lord charged you, to love the Lord your God, and to walk in all his ways, and to keep his commandments, and to cleave unto him, and to serve him with all your heart and with all your soul.

Joshua 22:5

I love the Lord, because he hath heard my voice and my supplications.

Psalm 116:1

A new commandment I give unto you, That ye love one another; as I have loved you, that ye also love one another.

By this shall all men know that ye are my disciples, if ye have love one to another.

John 13:34,35

Now as touching things offered unto idols, we know that we all have knowledge. Knowledge puffeth up, but charity edifieth.

1 Corinthians 8:1

Now the end of the commandment is charity out of a pure heart, and of a good conscience, and of faith unfeigned.

1 Timothy 1:5

And above all things have fervent charity among yourselves: for charity shall cover the multitude of sins.

1 Peter 4:8

He that loveth his brother abideth in the light, and there is none occasion of stumbling in him.
1 John 2:10

Finding Patience When You Need It

Rest in the Lord, and wait patiently for him: fret not thyself because of him who prospereth in his way, because of the man who bringeth wicked devices to pass.

Cease from anger, and forsake wrath: fret not thyself in any wise to do evil.

For evildoers shall be cut off: but those that wait upon the Lord, they shall inherit the earth.

Psalm 37:7-9

Better is the end of a thing than the beginning thereof: and the patient in spirit is better than the proud in spirit.

Be not hasty in thy spirit to be angry: for anger resteth in the bosom of fools.

Ecclesiastes 7:8,9

In your patience possess ye your souls.

Luke 21:19

And not only so, but we glory in tribulations also: knowing that tribulation worketh patience.

Romans 5:3

And let us not be weary in well doing: for in due season we shall reap, if we faint not.

Galatians 6:9

I therefore, the prisoner of the Lord, beseech you that ye walk worthy of the vocation wherewith ye are called.

Ephesians 4:1

With all lowliness and meekness, with longsuffering, forbearing one another in love.

Ephesians 4:2

That ye might walk worthy of the Lord unto all pleasing, being fruitful in every good work, and increasing in the knowledge of God;

Strengthened with all might, according to his glorious power, unto all patience and longsuffering with joyfulness.

Colossians 1:10,11

Now we exhort you, brethren, warn them that are unruly, comfort the feebleminded, support the weak, be patient toward all men.

1 Thessalonians 5:14

And the Lord direct your hearts into the love of God, and into the patient waiting for Christ.

2 Thessalonians 3:5

But thou, O man of God, flee these things; and follow after righteousness, godliness, faith, love, patience, meekness.

1 Timothy 6:11

That ye be not slothful, but followers of them who through faith and patience inherit the promises.

Hebrews 6:12

And so, after he had patiently endured, he obtained the promise.

Hebrews 6:15

For ye have need of patience, that, after ye have done the will of God, ye might receive the promise.

Hebrews 10:36

Wherefore seeing we also are compassed about with so great a cloud of witnesses, let us lay aside every weight, and the sin which doth so easily beset us, and let us run with patience the race that is set before us.

Hebrews 12:1

Knowing this, that the trying of your faith worketh patience.

But let patience have her perfect work, that ye may be perfect and entire, wanting nothing.

James 1:3,4

Wherefore, my beloved brethren, let every man be swift to hear, slow to speak, slow to wrath.

James 1:19

Be patient therefore, brethren, unto the coming of the Lord. Behold, the husbandman waiteth for the precious fruit of the earth, and hath long patience for it, until he receive the early and latter rain.

Be ye also patient; stablish your hearts: for the coming of the Lord draweth nigh.

James 5:7,8

And beside this, giving all diligence, add to your faith virtue; and to virtue knowledge;

And to knowledge temperance; and to temperance patience; and to patience godliness.

2 Peter 1:5,6

124

Here is the patience of the saints: here are they that keep the commandments of God, and the faith of Jesus.

Revelation 14:12

The Lord is not slack concerning his promise, as some men count slackness; but is longsuffering to us-ward, not willing that any should perish, but that all should come to repentance.

2 Peter 3:9

Finding Peace

When a man's ways please the Lord, he maketh even his enemies to be at peace with him.

Proverbs 16:7

It is an honour for a man to cease from strife: but every fool will be meddling.

Proverbs 20:3

And seek the peace of the city whither I have caused you to be carried away captives, and pray unto the Lord for it: for in the peace thereof shall ye have peace.

Jeremiah 29:7

Blessed are the peacemakers: for they shall be called the children of God.

Matthew 5:9

Acquaint now thyself with him, and be at peace: thereby good shall come unto thee.

Job 22:21

When he giveth quietness, who then can make trouble? and when he hideth his face, who then can behold him? whether it be done against a nation, or against a man only.

Job 34:29

Thou wilt keep him in perfect peace, whose mind is stayed on thee: because he trusteth in thee.

Trust ye in the Lord for ever: for in the Lord Jehovah is everlasting strength.

Isaiah 26:3,4

Lord, thou wilt ordain peace for us: for thou also hast wrought all our works in us.

Isaiah 26:12

What man is he that feareth the Lord? him shall he teach in the way that he shall choose.

His soul shall dwell at ease; and his seed shall inherit the earth.

Psalm 25:12,13

Mark the perfect man, and behold the upright: for the end of that man is peace.

Psalm 37:37

I will hear what God the Lord will speak: for he will speak peace unto his people, and to his saints: but let them not turn again to folly.

Psalm 85:8

Great peace have they which love thy law: and nothing shall offend them.

Psalm 119:165

They that trust in the Lord shall be as mount Zion, which cannot be removed, but abideth for ever.

Psalm 125:1

To whom he said, This is the rest wherewith ye may cause the weary to rest; and this is the refreshing: yet they would not hear.

Isaiah 28:12

The glory of this latter house shall be greater than of the former, saith the Lord of hosts: and in this place will I give peace, saith the Lord of hosts.

Haggai 2:9

My covenant was with him of life and peace; and I gave them to him for the fear wherewith he feared me, and was afraid before my name.

Malachi 2:5

To give light to them that sit in darkness and in the shadow of death, to guide our feet into the way of peace.

Luke 1:79

Peace I leave with you, my peace I give unto you: not as the world giveth, give I unto you. Let not your heart be troubled, neither let it be afraid.

John 14:27

Therefore being justified by faith, we have peace with God through our Lord Jesus Christ.

Romans 5:1

For the kingdom of God is not meat and drink; but righteousness, and peace, and joy in the Holy Ghost.

Romans 14:17

Be careful for nothing; but in every thing by prayer and supplication with thanksgiving let your requests be made known unto God.

And the peace of God, which passeth all understanding, shall keep your hearts and minds through Christ Jesus.

Philippians 4:6,7

And let the peace of God rule in your hearts, to the which also ye are called in one body; and be ye thankful.

Colossians 3:15

Now the Lord of peace himself give you peace always by all means. The Lord be with you all.

2 Thessalonians 3:16

He hath delivered my soul in peace from the battle that was against me: for there were many with me.

Psalm 55:18

Finding Strength

The Lord is my strength and song, and he is become my salvation: he is my God, and I will prepare him an habitation; my father's God, and I will exalt him.

Exodus 15:2

God is my strength and power: And he maketh my way perfect.

2 Samuel 22:23

The Lord is my strength and song, and is become my salvation.

Psalm 118:14

Behold, God is my salvation; I will trust, and not be afraid: for the Lord Jehovah is my strength and my song; he also is become my salvation.

Isaiah 12:2

For thou hast girded me with strength to battle: them that rose up against me hast thou subdued under me.

2 Samuel 22:40

It is God that girdeth me with strength, and maketh my way perfect.

Psalm 18:32

For thou hast girded me with strength unto the battle: thou hast subdued under me those that rose up against me.

Psalm 18:39

Let the words of my mouth, and the meditation of my heart, be acceptable in thy sight, O Lord, my strength, and my redeemer.

Psalm 19:14

The Lord will give strength unto his people; the Lord will bless his people with peace.

Psalm 29:11

Sing aloud unto God our strength: make a joyful noise unto the God of Jacob.

Psalm 81:1

My flesh and my heart faileth: but God is the strength of my heart, and my portion for ever.

Psalm 73:26

A wise man is strong; yea, a man of knowledge increaseth strength.

Proverbs 24:5

Trust ye in the Lord for ever: for in the Lord Jehovah is everlasting strength.

Isaiah 26:4

He giveth power to the faint; and to them that have no might he increaseth strength.

Isaiah 40:29

And he said unto me, My grace is sufficient for thee: for my strength is made perfect in weakness. Most gladly therefore will I rather glory in my infirmities, that the power of Christ may rest upon me.

2 Corinthians 12:9

Thy God hath commanded thy strength: strengthen, God, that which thou hast wrought for us.

Psalm 68:28

Finally, my brethren, be strong in the Lord, and in the power of his might.

Ephesians 6:10

Finding Wisdom When You Need It

That the God of our Lord Jesus Christ, the Father of glory, may give unto you the spirit of wisdom and revelation in the knowledge of him:

The eyes of your understanding being enlightened; that ye may know what is the hope of his calling, and what the riches of the glory of his inheritance in the saints,

And what is the exceeding greatness of his power to us-ward who believe, according to the working of his mighty power.

Ephesians 1:17-19

For this cause we also, since the day we heard it, do not cease to pray for you, and to desire that ye might be filled with the knowledge of his will in all wisdom and spiritual understanding.

Colossians 1:9

If any of you lack wisdom, let him ask of God, that giveth to all men liberally, and upbraideth not; and it shall be given him.

But let him ask in faith, nothing wavering. For he that wavereth is like a wave of the sea driven with the wind and tossed.

For let not that man think that he shall receive any thing of the Lord.

A double minded man is unstable in all his ways.

James 1:5-8

This wisdom descendeth not from above, but is earthly, sensual, devilish.

For where envying and strife is, there is confusion and every evil work.

But the wisdom that is from above is first pure, then peaceable, gentle, and easy to be entreated, full of mercy and good fruits, without partiality, and without hypocrisy.

And the fruit of righteousness is sown in peace of them that make peace.

James 3:15-18

He that loveth his brother abideth in the light, and there is none occasion of stumbling in him.

But he that hateth his brother is in darkness, and walketh in darkness, and knoweth not whither he goeth, because that darkness hath blinded his eyes.

1 John 2:10,11

Call unto me, and I will answer thee, and shew thee great and mighty things, which thou knowest not.

Jeremiah 33:3

But ye have an unction from the Holy One, and ye know all things.

1 John 2:20

But the anointing which ye have received of him abideth in you, and ye need not that any man teach you: but as the same anointing teacheth you of all things, and is truth, and is no lie, and even as it hath taught you, ye shall abide in him.

1 John 2:27

And thine ears shall hear a word behind thee, saying, This is the way, walk ye in it, when ye turn to the right hand, and when ye turn to the left.

Isaiah 30:21

Go not forth hastily to strive, lest thou know not what to do in the end thereof, when thy neighbour hath put thee to shame.
Debate thy cause with thy neighbour himself; and discover not a secret to another.

Proverbs 25:8,9

As an earring of gold, and an ornament of fine gold, so is a wise reprover upon an obedient ear.

Proverbs 25:12

I will instruct thee and teach thee in the way which thou shalt go: I will guide thee with mine eye.

Psalm 32:8

For with thee is the fountain of life: in thy light shall we see light.

Psalm 36:9

The entrance of thy words giveth light; it giveth understanding unto the simple.

Psalm 119:130

Turn you at my reproof: behold, I will pour out my spirit unto you, I will make known my words unto you.

Proverbs 1:23

For the Lord giveth wisdom: out of his mouth cometh knowledge and understanding.

He layeth up sound wisdom for the righteous: he is a buckler to them that walk uprightly.

Proverbs 2:6,7

O send out thy light and thy truth: let them lead me; let them bring me unto thy holy hill, and to thy tabernacles.

Psalm 43:3

Consider what I say; and the Lord give thee understanding in all things.

2 Timothy 2:7

Finding The Presence of God When You Do Not Feel It

And he said, My presence shall go with thee, and I will give thee rest.

Exodus 33:14

Teaching them to observe all things whatsoever I have commanded you: and, lo, I am with you always, even unto the end of the world.

Matthew 28:20

Let your conversation be without covetousness; and be content with such things as ye have: for he hath said, I will never leave thee, nor forsake thee.

Hebrews 13:5

A man that hath friends must shew himself friendly: and there is a friend that sticketh closer than a brother.

Proverbs 18:24

Greater love hath no man than this, that a man lay down his life for his friends.

Ye are my friends, if ye do whatsoever I command you.

Henceforth I call you not servants; for the servant knoweth not what his lord doeth: but I have called you friends; for all things that I have heard of my Father I have made known unto you.

John 15:13-15

Have not I commanded thee? Be strong and of a good courage; be not afraid, neither be thou dismayed: for the Lord thy God is with thee whithersoever thou goest.

Joshua 1:9

The Lord is nigh unto all them that call upon him, to all that call upon him in truth.

Psalm 145:18

But without faith it is impossible to please him: for he that cometh to God must believe that he is, and that he is a rewarder of them that diligently seek him.

Hebrews 11:6

All that the Father giveth me shall come to me; and him that cometh to me I will in no wise cast out.

John 6:37

Draw nigh to God, and he will draw nigh to you. Cleanse your hands, ye sinners; and purify your hearts, ye double minded.

James 4:8

Behold, I stand at the door, and knock: if any man hear my voice, and open the door, I will come in to him, and will sup with him, and he with me.

Revelation 3:20

And ye shall seek me, and find me, when ye shall search for me with all your heart.

Jeremiah 29:13

The Lord is good unto them that wait for him, to the soul that seeketh him.

Lamentations 3:25

Promises That God Will Always Hear You

And I have also heard the groaning of the children of Israel, whom the Egyptians keep in bondage; and I have remembered my covenant.
Exodus 6:5

If my people, which are called by my name, shall humble themselves, and pray, and seek my face, and turn from their wicked ways; then will I hear from heaven, and will forgive their sin, and will heal their land.
2 Chronicles 7:14

Thou shalt make thy prayer unto him, and he shall hear thee, and thou shalt pay thy vows.
Job 22:27

And they that know thy name will put their trust in thee: for thou, Lord, hast not forsaken them that seek thee.
Psalm 9:10

Lord, thou hast heard the desire of the humble: thou wilt prepare their heart, thou wilt cause thine ear to hear.
Psalm 10:17

The eyes of the Lord are upon the righteous, and his ears are open unto their cry.

The righteous cry, and the Lord heareth, and delivereth them out of all their troubles.
Psalm 34:15,17

Evening, and morning, and at noon, will I pray, and cry aloud: and he shall hear my voice.

Psalm 55:17

O thou that hearest prayer, unto thee shall all flesh come.

Psalm 65:2

Again I say unto you, That if two of you shall agree on earth as touching any thing that they shall ask, it shall be done for them of my Father which is in heaven.

For where two or three are gathered together in my name, there am I in the midst of them.

Matthew 18:19,20

For the Lord heareth the poor, and despiseth not his prisoners.

Psalm 69:33

Give ear, O Lord, unto my prayer; and attend to the voice of my supplications.

Psalm 86:6

He will regard the prayer of the destitute, and not despise their prayer.

Psalm 102:17

The Lord is nigh unto all them that call upon him, to all that call upon him in truth.

He will fulfil the desire of them that fear him: he also will hear their cry, and will save them.

Psalm 145:18,19

And it shall come to pass, that before they call, I will answer; and while they are yet speaking, I will hear.

Isaiah 65:24

Call unto me, and I will answer thee, and shew thee great and mighty things, which thou knowest not.

Jeremiah 33:3

And I will bring the third part through the fire, and will refine them as silver is refined, and will try them as gold is tried: they shall call on my name, and I will hear them: I will say, It is my people: and they shall say, The Lord is my God.

Zechariah 13:9

But thou, when thou prayest, enter into thy closet, and when thou hast shut thy door, pray to thy Father which is in secret; and thy Father which seeth in secret shall reward thee openly.

Be not ye therefore like unto them: for your Father knoweth what things ye have need of, before ye ask him.

Matthew 6:6,8

Promises for Protection

He that dwelleth in the secret place of the most High shall abide under the shadow of the Almighty.

I will say of the Lord, He is my refuge and my fortress: my God; in him will I trust.

Surely he shall deliver thee from the snare of the fowler, and from the noisome pestilence.

He shall cover thee with his feathers, and under his wings shalt thou trust: his truth shall be thy shield and buckler.

Thou shalt not be afraid for the terror by night; nor for the arrow that flieth by day;

Nor for the pestilence that walketh in darkness; nor for the destruction that wasteth at noonday.

A thousand shall fall at thy side, and ten thousand at thy right hand; but it shall not come nigh thee.

Only with thine eyes shalt thou behold and see the reward of the wicked.

Because thou hast made the Lord, which is my refuge, even the most High, thy habitation;

There shall no evil befall thee, neither shall any plague come nigh thy dwelling.

For he shall give his angels charge over thee, to keep thee in all thy ways.

They shall bear thee up in their hands, lest thou dash thy foot against a stone.

Thou shalt tread upon the lion and adder: the young lion and the dragon shalt thou trample under feet.

Because he hath set his love upon me, therefore will I deliver him: I will set him on high, because he hath known my name.

He shall call upon me, and I will answer him: I will be with him in trouble; I will deliver him, and honour him.

With long life will I satisfy him, and shew him my salvation.

Psalm 91:1-16

For this shall every one that is godly pray unto thee in a time when thou mayest be found: surely in the floods of great waters they shall not come nigh unto him.

Thou art my hiding place; thou shalt preserve me from trouble; thou shalt compass me about with songs of deliverance.

Psalm 32:6,7

God is our refuge and strength, a very present help in trouble.

Therefore will not we fear, though the earth be removed, and though the mountains be carried into the midst of the sea.

Psalm 46:1,2

As for God, his way is perfect; the word of the Lord is tried: he is a buckler to all them that trust in him.

2 Samuel 22:31

For the which cause I also suffer these things: nevertheless I am not ashamed: for I know whom I have believed, and am persuaded that he is able to keep that which I have committed unto him against that day.

2 Timothy 1:12

Now unto him that is able to keep you from falling, and to present you faultless before the presence of his glory with exceeding joy.

Jude 1:24

Promises For When You Need Healing

Surely he hath borne our griefs, and carried our sorrows: yet we did esteem him stricken, smitten of God, and afflicted.

But he was wounded for our transgressions, he was bruised for our iniquities: the chastisement of our peace was upon him; and with his stripes we are healed.

Isaiah 53:4,5

When the even was come, they brought unto him many that were possessed with devils: and he cast out the spirits with his word, and healed all that were sick:

That it might be fulfilled which was spoken by Esaias the prophet, saying, Himself took our infirmities, and bare our sicknesses.

Matthew 8:16,17

Who his own self bare our sins in his own body on the tree, that we, being dead to sins, should live unto righteousness: by whose stripes ye were healed.

1 Peter 2:24

Christ hath redeemed us from the curse of the law, being made a curse for us: for it is written, Cursed is every one that hangeth on a tree.

Galatians 3:13

And said, If thou wilt diligently hearken to the voice of the Lord thy God, and wilt do that which is right in his sight, and wilt give ear to his commandments, and keep all his statutes, I will put none of these diseases upon thee, which I have brought upon the Egyptians: for I am the Lord that healeth thee.

Exodus 15:26

And ye shall serve the Lord your God, and he shall bless thy bread, and thy water; and I will take sickness away from the midst of thee.

There shall nothing cast their young, nor be barren, in thy land: the number of thy days I will fulfil.

Exodus 23:25,26

There shall no evil befall thee, neither shall any plague come nigh thy dwelling.

Psalm 91:10

With long life will I satisfy him, and shew him my salvation.

Psalm 91:16

Bless the Lord, O my soul, and forget not all his benefits:

Who forgiveth all thine iniquities; who healeth all thy diseases.

Psalm 103:2,3

He sent his word, and healed them, and delivered them from their destructions.

Psalm 107:20

So shall my word be that goeth forth out of my mouth: it shall not return unto me void, but it shall accomplish that which I please, and it shall prosper in the thing whereto I sent it.

Isaiah 55:11

Every good gift and every perfect gift is from above, and cometh down from the Father of lights, with whom is no variableness, neither shadow of turning.

James 1:17

And, behold, there came a leper and worshipped him saying, Lord, if thou wilt, thou canst make me clean.

And Jesus put forth his hand, and touched him, saying, I will; be thou clean. And immediately his leprosy was cleansed.

Matthew 8:2,3

How God anointed Jesus of Nazareth with the Holy Ghost and with power: who went about doing good, and healing all that were oppressed of the devil; for God was with him.

Acts 10:38

The thief cometh not, but for to steal, and to kill, and to destroy: I am come that they might have life, and that they might have it more abundantly.
John 10:10

Jesus heard that they had cast him out; and when he had found him, he said unto him, Dost thou believe on the Son of God?
John 9:35

Jesus Christ the same yesterday, and to day, and for ever.
Hebrews 13:8

Verily, verily, I say unto you, He that believeth on me, the works that I do shall he do also; and greater works than these shall he do; because I go unto my Father.
John 14:12

Is any sick among you? let him call for the elders of the church; and let them pray over him, anointing him with oil in the name of the Lord:

And the prayer of faith shall save the sick, and the Lord shall raise him up; and if he have committed sins, they shall be forgiven him.
James 5:14,15

Promises For Deliverance

Truly my soul waiteth upon God: from him cometh my salvation.

He only is my rock and my salvation; he is my defence; I shall not be greatly moved.

Psalm 62:1,2

My soul, wait thou only upon God; for my expectation is from him.

He only is my rock and my salvation: he is my defence; I shall not be moved.

In God is my salvation and my glory: the rock of my strength, and my refuge, is in God.

Trust in him at all times; ye people, pour out your heart before him: God is a refuge for us.

Psalm 62:5-8

God hath spoken once; twice have I heard this; that power belongeth unto God.

Also unto thee, O Lord, belongeth mercy: for thou renderest to every man according to his work.

Psalm 62:11,12

And the Jews' passover was at hand, and Jesus went up to Jerusalem.

John 2:13

The Lord knoweth how to deliver the godly out of temptations, and to reserve the unjust unto the day of judgment to be punished.

2 Peter 2:9

He sent from above, he took me, he drew me out of many waters.

He delivered me from my strong enemy, and from them which hated me: for they were too strong for me.

They prevented me in the day of my calamity: but the Lord was my stay.

He brought me forth also into a large place; he delivered me, because he delighted in me.

Psalm 18:16-19

Thou shalt hide them in the secret of thy presence from the pride of man: thou shalt keep them secretly in a pavilion from the strife of tongues.

Psalm 31:20

I sought the Lord, and he heard me, and delivered me from all my fears.

Psalm 34:4

Many are the afflictions of the righteous: but the Lord delivereth him out of them all.

Psalm 34:19

Then said Jesus to those Jews which believed on him, If ye continue in my word, then are ye my disciples indeed;

And ye shall know the truth, and the truth shall make you free.

John 8:31,32

148

Then he called his twelve disciples together, and gave them power and authority over all devils, and to cure diseases.

Luke 9:1

And when he had called unto him his twelve disciples, he gave them power against unclean spirits, to cast them out, and to heal all manner of sickness and all manner of disease.

Matthew 10:1

Behold, I give unto you power to tread on serpents and scorpions, and over all the power of the enemy: and nothing shall by any means hurt you.

Luke 10:19

When the even was come, they brought unto him many that were possessed with devils: and he cast out the spirits with his word, and healed all that were sick:

That it might be fulfilled which was spoken by Esaias the prophet, saying, Himself took our infirmities, and bare our sicknesses.

Matthew 8:16,17

And the Lord shall deliver me from every evil work, and will preserve me unto his heavenly kingdom: to whom be glory for ever and ever.

2 Timothy 4:18

Overcoming Past Bad Memories

And be not conformed to this world: but be ye transformed by the renewing of your mind, that ye may prove what is that good, and acceptable, and perfect, will of God.

Romans 12:2

Therefore if any man be in Christ, he is a new creature: old things are passed away; behold, all things are become new.

2 Corinthians 5:17

Brethren, I count not myself to have apprehended: but this one thing I do, forgetting those things which are behind, and reaching forth unto those things which are before.

Philippians 3:13

Behold, I will do a new thing; now it shall spring forth; shall ye not know it? I will even make a way in the wilderness, and rivers in the desert.

Isaiah 43:19

Behold, the former things are come to pass, and new things do I declare: before they spring forth I tell you of them.

Isaiah 42:9

For, lo, the winter is past, the rain is over and gone.

Song of Solomon 2:11

Whom God hath set forth to be a propitiation through faith in his blood, to declare his righteousness for the remission of sins that are past, through the forbearance of God.

Romans 3:25

And be renewed in the spirit of your mind.

Ephesians 4:23

Being Close To God

The Lord is good unto them that wait for him, to the soul that seeketh him.

Lamentations 3:25

And ye shall seek me, and find me, when ye shall search for me with all your heart.

Jeremiah 29:13

Draw nigh to God, and he will draw nigh to you. Cleanse your hands, ye sinners; and purify your hearts, ye double minded.

James 4:8

But if from thence thou shalt seek the Lord thy God, thou shalt find him, if thou seek him with all thy heart and with all thy soul.

Deuteronomy 4:29

And he sought God in the days of Zechariah, who had understanding in the visions of God: and as long as he sought the Lord, God made him to prosper.

2 Chronicles 26:5

One thing have I desired of the Lord, that will I seek after; that I may dwell in the house of the Lord all the days of my life, to behold the beauty of the Lord, and to inquire in his temple.

For in the time of trouble he shall hide me in his pavilion: in the secret of his tabernacle shall he hide me; he shall set me up upon a rock.

And now shall mine head be lifted up above mine enemies round about me: therefore will I offer in his tabernacle sacrifices of joy; I will sing, yea, I will sing praises unto the Lord.

Hear, O Lord, when I cry with my voice: have mercy also upon me, and answer me.

When thou saidst, Seek ye my face; my heart said unto thee, Thy face, Lord, will I seek.

Psalm 27:4-8

As the hart panteth after the water brooks, so panteth my soul after thee, O God.

My soul thirsteth for God, for the living God: when shall I come and appear before God?

Psalm 42:1,2

O God, thou art my God; early will I seek thee: my soul thirsteth for thee, my flesh longeth for thee in a dry and thirsty land, where no water is;

To see thy power and thy glory, so as I have seen thee in the sanctuary.

Psalm 63:1,2

The Lord is nigh unto all them that call upon him, to all that call upon him in truth.

Psalm 145:18

For they got not the land in possession by their own sword, neither did their own arm save them: but thy right hand, and thine arm, and the light of thy countenance, because thou hadst a favour unto them.

Psalm 44:3

Blessed are they which do hunger and thirst after righteousness: for they shall be filled.

Matthew 5:6

That they should seek the Lord, if haply they might feel after him, and find him, though he be not far from every one of us.

Acts 17:27

And the Spirit and the bride say, Come. And let him that heareth say, Come. And let him that is athirst come. And whosoever will, let him take the water of life freely.

Revelation 22:17

PART II
MOTIVATION: IMPROVING YOUR SELF-IMAGE

By

Valerie Grant-Sokolosky

7
Go FOR IT!

Go for it! How often people who love and believe in me have encouraged me with those words. It wasn't always easy to put forth the effort to achieve success — to keep on keeping on. Hurts and disappointments have hit me, but nothing kept me from keeping on, even when there didn't seem to be any reason to continue.

Success may elude you for a season, a day, or a year, but then the right time comes when all of the circumstances seem to fall perfectly together. Adversity comes to everyone. You don't have to anticipate it or put it on your calendar. It will find you. The critical factor is how you respond to it when it hits.

My story is not one of continuous success, but one of many, many failures mixed with moments of success. We rarely read or hear that most winners fail much more often than they experience success. How can you spot a winner? She's the one who picks herself up and keeps going.

157

Two years ago I put together a television show on fashion tips. I took the idea to three stations. Two of the stations seemed interested and even allowed me to do a few shows, only to say later that they didn't have the budget to continue. I pursued my idea and then got a lucky break. No, not blind luck, but luck defined as preparedness meeting opportunity, mixed with faith.

A television station contacted me. They needed someone to do a fashions tips segment. I had already done several pilots for the other stations and was ready. I got the show!

A friend of mine enjoys putting together collages. She tells me that when all the pieces are cut out and strewn over the floor, there seems to be no possibility that they could ever fit together. Yet when the final picture is completed, a lovely scene is formed.

Life is learning to fit. In building a wardrobe you can combine an inexpensive item with the proper accessories to create an expensive-looking outfit. It's a matter of appropriately fitting the clothes and proper accessories together which makes the outfit work.

We need to fine tune ourselves to success — to make the right selections and to focus our direction on excellence. Be prepared when the opportunities open. Be ready for your season of success.

The Right Season: The Time Is Now!

What? *Me* start a new career after twenty years of devoting myself to being a wife and mother? *Me* step into a new career at the age of thirty-nine? It just can't be done. Especially not in the fashion-conscious city of Dallas. How could I make an impact in the field of fashion when so many long-time professionals have already made their mark for so many years?

For fourteen years I encased my life with raising my three precious children — changing diapers, going to PTA meetings, driving in car-pools, cooking, and keeping a household intact. I was completely dedicated to this life and, more importantly, I loved it! My husband had been busy making his mark in the business world. The thought of returning to a career had not even entered my mind until I found myself with a strange yearning to do something again in the fashion world. The children were older, no longer needing the bedtime tuck-ins and constant watching over. They had grown into three healthy, active teenagers who were no longer dependent on me. Their lives were filled with activities and friends.

''Lord, this just isn't right,'' I reasoned. ''I'm not supposed to have a career as long as the children are home.'' I really felt guilty even thinking of working. ''Lord, You've blessed me with such a lovely family; I should be completely content just meeting their needs. I've already had a glamorous career early in life. Please! If this desire for a career is not from You, and I can't imagine that it is, just take the desire away.''

The desire didn't leave. The yearning deep in my heart kept growing. Summer was approaching, and I had been invited to the Oregon coast. My husband was completely involved with his work. The children and I could visit the seashore and get away from the usual routine. This might be a good time to think things through clearly, get my head on straight, and realize this yearning of mine was just a fantasy. ''Great,'' I decided. ''We'll go!''

Excitedly, my two boys and daughter anticipated fun at the beach. We were eager for a solid rest and a time of relaxation. I was especially looking forward to having some quiet time, walking along the beach and talking to God. I hoped He would resound some wonderful wisdom right out of the waves.

While we were planning for our trip, a dear and discerning friend visiting me made this statement: ''Valerie, I have just the thing for you!'' She began sharing about a new career field called *image development*. ''It's related to the things you've done in the past, and it's a business all your own, something you can do part-time or however often you want.''

It sounded wonderful.

In Oregon I casually went into a bookstore and selected a book on color analysis. I started reading. Fascinated, I couldn't put it down. It described how to match your personal coloring of hair, skin, and eyes with complementary colors in your wardrobe to create a harmonious visual impact.

But I quickly became frustrated. The color analysis system presented exciting possibilities, but it also left me confused. It was categorized into four seasons. I was able to place myself in every one.

"I must be a woman for all seasons," I decided. "Am I a summer or a winter?" Some of the colors in each category seemed to look exactly right. As I became more frustrated with my lack of understanding, the desire to be trained in the color analysis business began to grow. Somehow I knew this training would be the beginning of my return into the image and personal development field.

When I returned home from my vacation, I discussed everything with my husband. He encouraged me, and I began looking for companies where I could receive training. Some of the companies I found were far away and some very expensive.

One day, a phone call came from a woman I didn't even know. She said, ''I understand you are looking into color-analysis training. I'm attending a meeting being held by a company who does training in this field. Would you like to go with me?''

I almost fell out of my chair. ''Of course,'' I said.

That was my answer to prayer. I said, ''Thanks, God! That's just like You to work that way.''

I became certified in color analysis. Soon after I began studying this field, I realized why I hadn't been able to figure out which ''season'' I was. Although the book I had read during my vacation had been instrumental in whetting my appetite for more knowledge, it had not included all the necessary information. I became exuberant, excited about the field I had always loved: clothing and fashion. I'd always enjoyed helping people look their best, and teaching image development gave me great fulfillment.

As I prepared to start my business, I questioned the Lord, ''Where will I find clients?'' I knew I couldn't pull people in from the street. ''I know,'' I thought. ''I'll begin with my friends.'' And I did.

As the weeks and months passed, I became absolutely engrossed with this new opportunity.

I started advertising and calling the newspapers to let them know what I was doing. I was excited about image development and shared with everyone how newsworthy I thought the field was.

Image development and color analysis were taking the country by storm. To my amazement my business began getting publicity. The first was a full-page article with a color picture in the fashion segment of the major Dallas paper!

Unbelievable! I thought. Yet I knew that all things are possible through God.

Then came an article about wardrobe consulting in *D Magazine,* one of the most highly respected magazines in Dallas. Next, a newspaper did a series of articles on image. Television opportunities on three of the local networks developed, with the programs "Your Best Colors" and "Your Image."

My husband was jogging one evening near our home when a neighbor stopped him. "Doug," he said, "I've certainly seen your wife's picture and articles about her in the papers a lot lately. Who is her P.R. agent?"

Doug laughed. We both knew that I have the best public relations agent there is — God. When He's for you, who can be against you?

As the years passed, my business grew. More and more people were becoming aware that this information would aid them in becoming all they can be and developing all that God has given them. It's never too late. God's timing is always perfect. He can do all things if we will only trust Him.

What is your dream? What is your heart's desire? What do you want to learn or achieve? Remember the definition of luck: preparedness meeting opportunity, mixed with faith.

Be prepared for your opportunities. My story is not unusual or similar success for you impossible. Success is attainable by anyone. The ingredients are the same: Decide what you want to do, set a goal for your career, and gain the knowledge or training you need to achieve your goal. Then *go for it!* Opportunities will come to you as you pursue your goal with a positive outlook and determination.

A friend recently asked me, "What is it that makes you strive so hard to achieve?"

I answered, "I never set goals that are unattainable, and I always intend to succeed."

Never give up: don't let setbacks stop you. When adversity comes, remember: it may knock you down, but it can't keep you down unless you allow it. Your season of success is predictable when you know God is for you, and you refuse to give up.

164

8
Exercises for excellence

Here are some exercises that will help you create your image of excellence and begin to establish an atmosphere of success in your life.

Imagine Yourself Successful

Always picture yourself successful. See the new you whom you desire to become. Set aside time each day to be alone and undisturbed. Get comfortable and relax completely. Close your eyes and reflect on where you are now and where you want to be in the future. See yourself in your new career, capable and full of self-confidence. Imagine every detail, and capture that picture in your mind. When discouragements come throughout the day, pull that image up in your mind and look at it.

Remember Your Past Successes

Rehearse your past successes. Never minimize any success you have experienced, no matter how small that success may seem. Write down your successes. You will be surprised how much a well-kept diary will encourage you when things don't seem to be going your way. Look back and remember your successes. Develop the habit of focusing your attention on these. Everything we do in life can become a habit, either good or bad. Maintaining a habit of focusing on the positive somehow generates even more positive experiences.

Forget the Failures

What do we do with the failures? They are real, too. If we're smart and care about our own well-being, we'll learn from the failures, then *forget them.* Dwelling on past failures causes ''loser's syndrome.''

Instead, pick yourself up, dust yourself off, and keep striving for that *image of excellence.* Just as there are seasons of success, there are also times when failure can be caused by wrong timing and uncontrollable circumstances. Take responsibility for your life, but not for the failures. Learn from them, but don't be overcome by them.

Celebrate Your Successes

No matter how minor they may seem to be, celebrate your successes! They need to be celebrated. Your successes are your memory makers.

When your child comes home with a good grade, celebrate it. When you make that sale, take the family to dinner. When your husband is promoted, buy a meaningful card and use candles on the table. Think of ways that are your very own. Each celebration will make a marker for remembering your successes.

Not long ago my family seemed to hit nothing but brick walls. It was happening to each one of us: my husband, my children, and me. Projects we tried to develop couldn't get off the ground. Sales we needed to generate weren't coming in. Opportunities seemed far away, and doors always closed to us. Finally, we sat down together and discussed the situation. We all agreed that we appeared to be completely surrounded by brick walls. But as we talked through this, we realized we had to make a decision. The choice was ours. We could either give up or keep on. Because our habit of keeping on and encouraging one another was established, the choice was made.

The past successes were there telling us, ''You've made it in the past, you can do it again.'' We decided to shoot for the moon and believe we would at least land among the stars. Not long after we made this definite decision, opportunities opened and the seasons of success began again. We celebrated each success as it came.

Set Definite Goals

Nothing happens by accident. Opportunities come, but you would never be ready for them if you didn't have a clear direction and already knew where you wanted to go. Setting goals *does* make the difference.

From the beginning of our marriage, my husband and I have set goals. While the children were still young, we started including them in a goal-setting exercise we do at least once a year.

On New Year's Eve, we celebrate together and reflect on what has happened during the past year. Then we dream, hope, and plan for the next year. Each of us writes on a piece of paper three definite, attainable goals for our mental, spiritual, and physical life. I put these in an envelope and seal it. On the following New Year's Eve we open the envelope. It's exciting and fun to see if the goals have been fulfilled.

Respond Positively to Life

This final exercise is for developing a positive self-image and response to life. Each of us has an image of ourself that is the result of unconscious reactions to past experiences, successes, or failures. Our minds are like sensitive computers. What we put into our computer determines our future response to life.

168

I have a friend who remembers rainy days as wonderful moments in her childhood. Her mother baked goodies on those days. When my friend came home from school, she smelled the sweet aroma of a freshly baked pie or cake. She does the same for her family. To this day she loves what to me are dreary, rainy days.

I always disliked rainy days, because I couldn't go out and play. I was an only child and wanted to be around other children all the time. I'm still a people person. My computer was programmed negatively about rainy days. I can now change my response because I have insight.

There are so many things in this world which are completely beyond your control. But your image, your positive reactions to life, and your decisions are completely within your control. Change the input and thus control the output.

''Part II'' is from *Seasons of Success* by Valerie Grant-Sokolosky (Tulsa: Honor Books, 1985), pp. 15-22, 25-28.

Part III
Protocol
IN BUSINESS

By

Valerie Grant-Sokolosky

9
RELATIONSHIPS
IN BUSINESS

Today one of the most common concerns among men is, "How am I supposed to treat a woman who is now my business equal?" and for women, "Should I expect the traditional female courtesies when I am an executive?"

Because women have been achieving high levels of success, the role of the female has changed. No longer is she employed only as a secretary, but also as a boss and peer. This puts a whole new code of conduct into effect among the office staff as to how to treat women in the day-to-day activities at work.

You as a woman can and should set the stage for how you *want* to be treated. If you expect equal pay and equal status on the job, you should also expect to be treated as an equal in other areas. For instance, a woman should be willing to open a door first if she arrives there before a man whether it is during or after work hours. However, if a man and woman arrive at the door

173

at the same time, the man still opens the door. A woman should realize that a man often enjoys holding the door for her, and she can non-verbally indicate to him whether he should.

This mutual admiration society approach within the office can lessen the strain of doing something just because you are female.

In today's business world, the male/female relationships at work tend to be looked upon as those of colleagues, not as sex-oriented. This works well as long as both the man and woman feel comfortable in letting go of some previous manners taught, such as the woman expecting the man to help her with her coat or to always open the door for her. (Today a female employee can open the door for a senior executive unless he moves forward to open it for her.) Common sense should be used when it comes to such issues.

Handling Sexual Advances

This seems to be a problem not only with men approaching women, but with aggressive women approaching men. A good rule of thumb is to not give *any* suggestion of interest when an overture is obvious. It *does* take two to start any relationship.

Such things as a lingering eye contact or a handshake held too long can give cues without a word being said. If someone makes eye contact and lingers with a smile, simply look away and break that eye contact. If a man shakes hands and continues to "hold" hands, just take one step back. Your hand must follow and it will break the handshake.

If you are actually approached verbally, try reacting with humor rather than making an issue. Talking about your spouse or current date can discourage an attraction.

The important thing to remember is that relationships can begin very innocently with kind remarks and invitations to lunch or dinner.

Here are some professional ethics to keep in mind:

• Never accept advances of any kind from a married person.

• Dating clients is dangerous and unprofessional unless the business relationship has come to an end and the social part of the relationship can be free from interfering with business.

• Dating the boss is awkward and inappropriate.

Male Customer's Compliments and Advances

As far as handling a male client's compliments, a simple "thank you" is all that is necessary. Handling advances can be done two ways — with humor or by ignoring them. Always remain gracious and professional and do not give any non-verbal clues of being interested.

In addition, try thinking of yourself as a professional who happens to be a woman rather than a woman who is trying to be professional. You will find that as you put this into practice, your response to these situations will be natural and effective without being offensive or unfeminine.

Refusing a Lunch Invitation

Refusing a luncheon with someone is your perogative, whether in or outside of business. If you truly feel that a man has ulterior motives in asking you to lunch, you can simply state that you would prefer meeting at your office where your information is more readily available.

When you feel hesitant about going to lunch with a male client for this reason, it is probably better in the long run not to give any opportunity for misunderstood intentions. Keeping everything within business hours and the business setting is always appropriate.

The Role of the Female

Addressing the Female Peer

There are several names that should *not* be used by a man or another woman in referring to or addressing a woman: "girl," "dear," and "honey" are just a few.

Once when giving a presentation to a group of women, the speaker referred to them as "girls." Nothing was said at the time, but later she received a phone call from one of the women who had attended.

The attendee said, "If you don't mind my making a suggestion, don't ever call women 'girls.' It's demeaning. I have other friends in the business world who also dislike it. We're not girls — we're women." I have heard many comments from women executives that they just do not like being called "girls" under any circumstances.

If a man seems to be acting condescendingly toward you by calling you "honey," consider the man's attitude before you react. Some men have formed this habit long ago, see nothing wrong with it, and do not mean any disrespect by it. In this case, "honey" does not reflect how the man feels about you professionally. However, if you feel that the man is being condescending, do one of the following:

- Ignore what he said.

- Say, "My name is _____."

- Revert to calling him Mr._____.

- Continue the business conversation and stick to facts.

Female/Female Relationships

The old idiom "It's lonely at the top" is true. Within any organization, there are defined levels. You cannot fully participate in two levels at the same time. You are either in management or on the support staff. You have to make a choice. You cannot maintain your identity at one level if you associate more comfortably and more obviously on another level. In other words, you cannot maintain a professional distance and be "one of the daily lunch group."

Many women in support roles have levels of informal power in the company. A secretary or receptionist can control whether you talk to her boss on the phone or get an appointment with him, she can relay your messages in a negative or positive manner, or she can fail to notify you of an important meeting. If you develop a good business relationship with her, she can pass on valuable tips to help you deal with her boss.

When dealing with a female who is in a lower position than you:

• Don't act condescendingly or demeaningly toward her.

• Don't patronize her or preach to her on how she should try for a more important position.

• Never confide any of your personal problems or matters to her and try to avoid

178

learning any intimate details of her personal life. Keep all such conversations at a superficial level.

Wives of Male Associates

The wives may be concerned with potential intimate situations especially during out-of-town trips. Female business associates are sharing something with their husbands that wives cannot share in — his work. Keep this in mind whenever you are around the wives. Always be friendly and treat them with courtesy.

Entertaining a Male Client

A woman entertaining a male client can create an awkward situation unless she sets the mood and arranges the meeting appropriately. Some men may still be uncomfortable with women initiating the invitation. Here are a few suggestions to make things go smoothly for both parties:

1. When calling the man, make sure you tell him clearly that you would like to take him to lunch to discuss business. Say something like this, ''Bob, I'd like to take you to lunch and we can discuss this further.'' Or make the request in a neutral way by asking the client to let your company treat him to lunch. The woman executive is then seen as an agent of the company and not as a woman asking a man to lunch.

2. It is preferable to choose a restaurant you go to often, ideally a club where your company owns a membership, and arrange ahead of time for the bill not to be brought to the table. Make the reservation in your name, and give the restaurant your credit card number ahead of time. Quickly excuse yourself during dessert and coffee to sign the check, or sign on the way out.

3. If you go to a restaurant where the bill must be brought to the table, simply quietly ask the waiter to have the check brought to you. Use a credit card to pay it. If the man insists on paying, it is best to let him, rather than make an issue of who should pay. If lunch meetings are frequent, you may want to alternate paying. (Incidentally, after signing a credit card receipt, pull off both carbons. This will eliminate any possibility of figure changes which might be made after you leave.)

4. Tipping should be added to include the usual 15 percent and perhaps an extra $1 or $2 if the headwaiter has been extra helpful.

5. If your colleague orders a cocktail, never feel you will offend him by ordering a Perrier or other non-alcoholic beverage. If you do not drink because of personal convictions, you should never feel second best because you choose not to drink.

Lunching with Other Women Employees

Decide ahead of time who will be in charge of the bill and pay the person your portion plus the tip when the bill arrives. Be very careful to do this quickly and generously. There is nothing more irritating to a waiter and to other women who are in a hurry to get back to work than to have to wait impatiently while someone tries to figure a portion of the bill to the penny.

Taking Another Woman to Lunch

If as a woman you call to ask another woman to have lunch with you, you should intend to pay the bill.

Be especially gracious in ordering as the guest of an entrepreneur. Remember, a business owner is *not* on a corporate account. Be respectful that prices may affect her company profit in a different way. (Incidentally, no matter what company your client is with, always order a moderately priced item unless he or she specifically suggests something expensive. Expense accounts are well monitored these days.)

The Corporate Wife

Leigh and her husband were planning to go to a reception of another company in order to get to know the people for business purposes. It was a very important occasion. My friend's husband was out of town and, due to bad weather, could not fly home in time to go to the reception.

Leigh certainly did not want to go without him, yet even without being able to talk to him about the situation, she knew that meeting the people at that reception was important to him. Leigh decided she would go alone. She chose an outfit that was conservative, but appropriate, and went.

At the reception, she introduced herself and explained that even though her husband had been detained, she had wanted to come alone to meet the people.

Making this special effort was one of the nicest things Leigh could have done for her husband. He asked her all kinds of questions about whom she had met and what the people were like. Also, the other company people were impressed to realize that the man's wife was so special. This woman knew what to do to support her husband in the way he needed it.

Behind a successful man is often a loving and supportive woman. Your role as your husband's support becomes more important the farther up the ladder of success he climbs. But how can you feel comfortable entertaining his clients and/or business colleagues? Here are some guidelines in the art of entertaining for you to follow and be a gracious hostess always:

• When planning to entertain and you feel a need for assistance from your husband's staff, ask your husband whom to contact and what responsibilities can be shared with you.

• Familiarize yourself with the business your husband is in and be able to speak the language when around his colleagues and clients. If he is in the high-tech industry, you should know the difference between hardware and software; in real estate, know something about the general market and interest rates; in advertising, understand market share, prime time, and layouts.

• Stay well read and knowledgeable about what is going on in your country, your city, and internationally.

• Stay informed of the latest fashions and continually upgrade your image to go along with his. Be sure you wear clothes that are currently in style and are appropriate to the occasion. Update your hairstyle and make-up periodically. Always reflect the best image you can for your husband's sake and yours.

• Celebrate his successes with a surprise candlelight dinner just for you two or an unannounced weekend getaway.

• Stay in good physical shape and get plenty of rest.

Mary, a very dear and special friend, is the epitome of a successful corporate wife. I asked her what she thought was the most important thing she does for her husband. She said, ''I try to remember I'm not just a support to my husband, but rather I'm part of a team.''

Mary has learned that his success becomes *their* success and together they share the reward.

10
TRAVELING WITH COLLEAGUES OR ALONE

Traveling With a Senior Executive

As a junior executive, you should aide a senior executive as much as possible. Assist with details such as checking in and out of the hotel and tipping. Do not engage the senior executive in long conversations unless he encourages you.

When getting into a car or limousine, wait to take a seat until the senior executive has chosen one first.

When flying on a corporate jet, always arrive early. Board after the senior executive or host, and sit where you are shown. Do not ask for refreshments unless they are offered. Be neat when eating and drinking and do not litter.

Always thank the crew as you leave. Write a thank you note to the executive who reserved you a seat on the flight.

Male and Female Colleagues Traveling Together

When men and women travel together on business, certain behavior should be followed for the sake of reputation. Here are some basic guidelines.

1. Avoid flirtations, no matter how innocent. They may be misunderstood.

2. At the first sign of inappropriate behavior on the part of your colleague, take some action to end it right there. Then act as though the incident never happened to preserve the working relationship.

3. When business needs to be conducted, arrange to work in a public place such as the hotel lobby or restaurant.

4. A man and a woman should be separately responsible for expenses.

• A woman executive should travel with advance money or use her own money to pay for her expenses, then later be reimbursed by her company.

• If a male and female colleague dine together, they should each use their own expense account to pay for their meal.

• A woman executive should tip for her own baggage handling and airport limousine fee.

186

• Either the man or woman may pay shared taxi fares, then reimbursements should be made for filing individual expense reports.

A Woman Traveling Alone on Business

Business travel is a special concern for women. Your travel objectives, however, are the same as for the male executive. You have a job to do and you want to do that job efficiently, minimizing time, energy, cost, and aggravation while maximizing your comfort and enjoyment.

Safety/Danger Zones and Times

When traveling alone, establish safety/danger zones and times. For instance:

Safety zones — your hotel room, the front desk, the coffee shop.

Danger zones — the bar, elevators, stairways, parking lot, garages, and hallways. While in these areas, stay alert to signs of danger.

Safety times — daylight. Make your flight reservations early in the day and arrive at your destination before dark.

Dining

Many women who travel tell me that they do not feel comfortable dining alone in a restaurant and, for that reason, often use room service. By eating in their room, they accomplish more work, but often would rather be among people.

As a businesswoman, you have every right to dine alone in a restaurant. Walk in confidently and say, "Dinner for one, please." The key is to act as if you belong there and deserve the same good service given to everyone else.

If the service is good, leave a tip of 15 to 20 percent. Also keep in mind when figuring the tip that there is no such thing as a table for one. If your waiter had served two people, the check would have been twice as much and the tip would have been twice as big.

If you intend to be left alone while dining, try the following:

1. Remain businesslike in your dress and behavior. You could even carry your briefcase or other papers. Both actions clearly give the message that you are a professional businesswoman and are involved in reviewing business while you are eating.

2. Handle intrusions diplomatically.

If someone you are not interested in talking to starts talking to you, smile pleasantly and answer him, then take papers from your briefcase and begin working.

If someone asks to join you and you want to refuse, simply say, "No thanks."

If you prefer not to travel alone, look into traveling with someone else in your organization or with a group. You might be able to travel with other females from other companies who are going to the same place at the same time.

Hotels

Precautions

When staying in a hotel or motel, both men and women should take certain precautions, but women should be especially careful.

1. Avoid exposing your room number in a public setting such as in a restaurant when signing your check.

2. Always double lock your room door and put on the chain. Check balcony doors and windows. If one is broken or cannot be locked, call for a maintenance man to fix it or show you how to lock it.

3. Do not enter your room if people are standing idly nearby. Walk past your door, then return later. When leaving your room, look carefully down the hallway as a precaution. Always check to be sure the door has locked behind you.

Tipping

When checking out of a hotel, tip the bellman $1 per bag or $1 for the first bag and $.50 for smaller bags. Rather than tipping per bag, you may give a general tip of $3 to $5.

Tip the valet attendant who brings your car $2 minimum — $1 for bringing the car and $1 per bag.

11
Planning Corporate Entertainment

The days of the unlimited expense account are no longer the norm. Corporations are cutting back in every financial area. For this reason, they are watching more closely the business person's expense account. Highly visible business entertainment, weekend getaways, and inclusion of family and friends are no longer common.

When done correctly, entertaining is one of the most productive tools available to the business person. Billions of dollars are spent each year for entertaining to create additional business for the company. Business entertaining is not just fun — it is profitable. Cost effectiveness of entertaining *is* a consideration.

Reasons for Entertaining

1. To form relationships which will lead toward further business between two companies.

2. To express gratitude. Treating someone to an expensive formal dinner or even a simple lunch is a good way of saying, "Thank you."

3. To celebrate a business success. Reward yourself and others for a job well done.

4. To help make decisions. Sometimes getting away from the office atmosphere allows people to think more openly and objectively when a difficult decision needs to be made.

The Key Ingredient

Careful planning is the key ingredient to successful entertaining. There are so many details that it is important to write everything down.

Make sure you have remembered to arrange every detail as well as to remember what details you have arranged! Your written plans can be a valuable resource when you analyze the success of your business entertaining and plan future events, whether large or small. In planning a party consider: business objectives, cost, and time commitment.

Tips for the Good Host

Being considerate of your guests is the most important prerequisite for any host or hostess.

Mary, who entertains frequently with her executive husband, has learned to plan events and allow enough time for people's relaxation as well. Packing an agenda full of entertaining is not relaxing or fun without including personal time for them to do what they choose.

There are certain how-to's that apply to every situation in which you will entertain:

• Select a location for the event which will be comfortable for the guests. The area should be cool and well ventilated. Music should be pleasant and soft.

• Plan the arrangement of the buffet table and beverage service areas, and the seating and reception line to facilitate the movement of guests.

• See that adequate serving utensils, napkins, and other service items are available.

• Consult with your caterer to determine the types and amount of beverages to serve for the length of the party and the tastes of your guests.

• Select tablecloths, napkins, floral arrangements, and serving pieces that are interesting. Arrange dishes, utensils, and serving pieces artfully on the table.

• Use as many flowers as your budget will allow. A good florist will help you enhance the table decor.

The Always Rules

• Treat every guest as a VIP (very important person).

• Always ask if your guests would like to participate in a certain activity you have planned.

• Plan events that you know your guests will enjoy. For example, some guests may prefer a Western barbecue to a formal sit-down dinner.

• Be sure there is sufficient room and plenty of chairs.

• Offer a variety of beverages.

• If you notice that a guest is not touching some of his food, ask him if he would like more of the items that he has eaten. Never put your guest on the spot by asking him why he has not eaten something.

• Food, beverages, service, and entertainment should be top quality.

• To cut down on expenses, invite fewer guests, select less-expensive foods, or serve fewer courses — *never* sacrifice quality.

Be a gracious host! Smile. Mingle with your guests. Visit with everyone. Introduce newcomers and see that shy guests are put at ease.

• In your home, provide the restrooms with guest towels, fancy soaps, and other special items.

• Never make an issue of something that went wrong in front of your guests.

• Make sure that your dishes, utensils, and serving pieces sparkle.

• All service personnel should be impeccably groomed. Uniforms should be spotless and pressed. Hair and nails must be well manicured.

Menu Planning

Because food is the most important component of a successful formal meal, the menu should be planned with great care.

The number of courses you serve is dependent upon the importance of the occasion and the size of your budget. Naturally, for very important affairs, prepare the most elaborate meal you can afford. A formal luncheon should consist of two to three courses and a formal dinner, of three to seven courses.

Two to Seven Course Meals

Two Course Meal
1. Salad, vegetable, meat
2. Dessert

Three Course
1. Appetizer or soup
2. Salad, vegetable, meat
3. Dessert

195

Four Course
1. Appetizer or soup
2. Salad
3. Vegetable, meat
4. Dessert

Five Course
1. Appetizer
2. Soup
3. Salad
4. Vegetable, meat
5. Dessert

Six Course
1. Appetizer
2. Soup
3. Fish
4. Vegetable, meat
5. Green salad and cheese
6. Dessert

Seven Course
1. Appetizer
2. Soup
3. Fish
4. Sorbet
5. Vegetable, meat
6. Green salad and cheese
7. Dessert

• Make sure your menu is suitable for your guests' appetites and tastes, the type of event, and the time of day and year. Serve hearty, hot dishes in the winter and light, cool ones in the summer. Never serve finger food and dainties to a group of men or *steak tartare* to a group of women.

• Select foods within your budget. Berries out of season should not be added. If you need to watch your budget, select easily attainable foods.

• The food must awaken the taste buds and please the eye.

• Select as many fresh foods as possible.

• Plan nutritious meals. Avoid fried or heavily sauced foods.

• Select foods with a variety of tastes, colors, textures, and temperatures.

• Since many people are controlling serious health problems with special diets, the wise host should ask his guests if they have any special dietary restrictions. This can be conveniently done when extending invitations or receiving RSVP's by telephone.

''Part III'' is from *Corporate Protocol — A Brief Case for Business Etiquette* by Valerie Grant-Sokolosky (Tulsa: Harrison House, 1986), pp. 97-102, 167-176, 195-199.

Part IV
For the working mother

By

Edwin Louis Cole

and

Nancy Corbett Cole

12
Two careers:
BUSINESS AND MOTHER

While contemplating ministry in the home and motherhood, I happened to be on the telephone talking to my daughter, Lois. She and her husband, Rick, have given us two of the most beautiful, brilliant, loveable and enjoyable granddaughters the world has ever seen. And if you think I am prejudiced, you are right!

While I was talking to her, I asked her what being a mother meant to her. This was her reply: "Being a mother means never having a free moment even on vacations. It means being responsible for little people twenty-four hours a day with never a day off."

I chimed in with the observation that even when our children are in their thirties, as Lois is, the responsibility is still there. We both laughed. She and I enjoy motherhood. I do not know of anyone who enjoys her children more or is a better mother without stress or strain than Lois. However, the fact of the matter is that we touched on a sober reality: motherhood is a full-time job that never ends! Being a mother is a great and awesome responsibility. Many of us get married and can hardly wait for that first baby. All we can think of is that soft warm, tiny mass of humanity.

What women usually do not think about are the sleepless nights, the mounds of dirty diapers, the feeding difficulties, the colic, and all those other unpleasant things that rear their ugly heads during the course of infancy and the toddler stage.

''Will this ever end?'' may be a mother's cry! The answer is obvious. Barring calamity, no it will never end. But the joys of motherhood far outweigh the burden of responsibility.

Mothers imprint their attitudes and ideas onto the child's young, immature life. So it is very important what we are putting into that child. Are you implanting a fearful, critical attitude or a peaceful, loving, forgiving, God-fearing nature?

When my children were young, I guess I made every mistake a new mother can make. I am sure I was short-tempered at times. None of us is perfect. But, *it is what we do with our failures that counts.* Do we take them to the Lord and ask for forgiveness? Do we ask our children to forgive us when necessary?

Our attitudes toward the children and the constancy of living a godly life day by day are what will stay in their minds and hearts. That is what will give them a security in their identity to carry them through the crises and good times of later years. Providing you have worked on putting a God-consciousness into their spirits, they will have the marvelous assurance of who they are in God.

Also remember that each of your children has a different, unique personality. When Paul, as a young teenager, spent hours playing the guitar in his room, I had no idea he was composing songs that later blessed our congregation and others with their purity and simplicity.

Nor did I recognize Lois' propensity for debate (which sometimes we called ''arguing'') that presaged a successful career as a prosecuting attorney.

With Joann, I remember seeing her tie her shoes at a very early age, before kindergarten, and I was ashamed that I had not even tried to teach her that skill which she learned by herself. Then in fifth grade, there was talk of skipping her to seventh grade. I realized she was smart, but what I did not realize was her extraordinary sensitivity to the world around her. Not until she was through school and going through a turbulent time spiritually did I develop an awareness that she, and the other children were made up of spirit, soul and body, each uniquely different from the others.

My children still surprise me with some of the qualities they exhibit. I think, ''Where did they ever learn that?'' We have to remember we may not always see our children as they really are in God's eyes. We must discipline ourselves in prayer to learn what ''makes them tick.''

Edwin and I do not have a perfect family, but we have stayed on our knees and God has been faithful. If you think you, or your children, cannot live up to God's greatest goals for your lives, quit trying to do it on your own. Let God be strong within you, instead of trying to be strong for Him. We cannot impress God. But we are impressed by Him when we see what He makes of our lives. Release your children to God and allow them to achieve.

My daughters have struggled with being working mothers as I did. I have noticed, however, that every woman in Scripture worked or held some kind of title, although not always for pay. Every mother must examine her own heart about working outside the home, whether as a volunteer or for pay. What a fallacy to call a full-time homemaker a nonworking mother!

There are women who prefer outside involvement, even though they do not have to work. The Bible certainly teaches it is better to be busy than idle and that godly women adorn themselves with good works. Idleness leads to gossip. It also leads to fantasy and sexual immorality. So the choice of occupying yourself with work or not is up to you, although the priorities of family first never change.

If you find yourself in the workplace earning a living for any reason, then by all means, get the best job possible, preferably one with a chance for advancement. If you have the talent and brains for a high-level job and the opportunity is there, then go for it! If you have to be away from your family anyway, at least make those hours worth your time, and theirs.

There is a pitfall in career planning, however, which you will have to keep in balance — and that is the cost to your family.

Lois was in line for a promotion but in observing the people already in that coveted post, she saw this would be a very time-consuming position that would require long hours both in the office and at home. She had had a taste of this occasionally and it troubled her. Once when she was engaged in some extra, very intensive work, she told me that even though she would go home to be with her family, she was so preoccupied, she would not hear them when they attempted to converse with her. In one instance her troubled little girl said, ''Mom! I have asked you the same question five times, and you didn't hear me even once.''

When the time came for the promotion, Lois very prayerfully and conscientiously turned it down. Since then, she and Rick have moved to an entirely new community where their workplaces are closer to home and their daughters' schools, and Lois is in an even more exciting position! God does lead and guide us, as He has promised in His Word.

Whether you are working or not, every mother wonders at times if she is losing patience or sanity. A few years ago, I was visiting my son when his youngest child was barely three years old. My daughter-in-law, Judi, was being a lovely hostess and making sure I was comfortable.

The first morning she scurried around the kitchen serving waffles to us all. When she handed me my plate, I looked down at a sight that would make a pre-schooler drool: buttered waffles covered with syrup and cut into bite-sized pieces. When Judi saw me hesitate, she looked at the plate and realized what she had done. We all laughed uproariously. Cutting everyone's food is the classic blooper of a mother of small children!

Judi found that being home continually with her children caused her mind to stagnate and her social skills to diminish. So she worked sporadically, choosing her own hours as a makeup artist, and finally started a business out of her own house. Now she is able to be with the children but have outside interests as well.

A mother with young children must be careful lest the cares of the world choke the life, or spirit out of her. When the pressure is on, it is easy to develop bad habits. One of those is to take out frustrations on the children. We must learn to accept our weaknesses as ours and not blame the children because we have let anxiety or pressure mount.

On the other hand, we cannot wait and let the father deal with the more serious issues. ''Just wait until your father gets home!'' is a phrase that, with a little bit of contemplation and calmness, could so often be avoided. A working father comes home from a turbulent world wanting a peaceful haven. He does not need his children dreading his return home, nor does he need a blow-by-blow account of every detail of the day.

The relationship with your children must never become a stumbling block to the relationship with your husband. Children need the benefits of a good marriage between their father and mother.

A common complaint among young mothers is the massive amount of work — cleaning up after more and more people in the house, mounds of laundry, hungry mouths to feed three times a day. Most young mothers lead strenuous lives. But if you plan carefully, and train the children (and your husband!) to help, you can do it. I was surprised to read a doctor's report suggesting that by eight years of age children should be responsible for cleaning their own bedrooms, and by ten they should be able to do any major chore around the house, even vacuuming.

I discovered this for myself when my children were very small. Many a night as we pioneered a new church with three children under four years of age, I crawled into bed on legs that felt hollowed out and barely functionable. I will never forget the feeling! Then Edwin began ministering as a missionary-evangelist and was frequently away on trips that lasted days, weeks, and sometimes months. To add to the difficulty of being alone with the children, I worked full time and drove an hour each way to work. Those were not easy years, but God gave me wisdom.

I realized that if I wanted the children to help me with chores when they were older, I might as well start right then. (Later I discovered this was scriptural! — Hebrews 12:11.) So on Saturday mornings, they each had an assignment. Even the youngest at five years old had a dust cloth and dusted the entire house herself. Granted, I had to go behind them and pick up what they missed after they were in bed at night, but after a few years of investing this way, I reaped big dividends. They all became valuable helps to me around the house.

There is only one regret that remains from those years, and that is when Paul showed an interest in cooking, I did not teach him. (Yes, I confess to stereotyped thinking!) Not only did I live to regret stifling that creative outlet, but so does his wife, Judi!

Another thing God showed me during that time was how to spend time alone with Him regardless of how full my days were. The plan He gave me was both simple and effective once I implemented it. Here it is: I put the children to bed earlier!

I knew Paul had a flashlight under his covers and he was reading, and I could hear Lois and Joann giggling. Nevertheless, I was marvelously alone for a few quiet moments in the evenings to enjoy the Lord — just Him and me. That relationship is the most important to keep intact.

As Edwin says, "It is more important to talk to the Lord about your children than to your children about the Lord."

One more thing I want to add: Did you ever treat your child or children in a way you had vowed never to treat them? Perhaps your parents treated you that way, and long ago you vowed you would never do the same thing. If this has happened to you, examine your heart for unforgiveness toward your parents. You may hardly be aware of the resentment that you still feel over those incidents that disturbed you. When you become aware of hidden resentments, you can be released by forgiving those who hurt you, whether they are still living or not, and asking the Lord to take it out of your life.

Overall, it is your attitude toward your child that will linger on. An attitude of appreciation toward children is what I suggest as the antidote for attitudes of resentment, jealousy, or frustration. Choose to appreciate the great attributes God has placed within the life of each one.

Thank God every day for your husband and/or children. They are His gifts to you. Thank Him for your home. Thank Him for the peace that He floods your heart with. Psalm 91, Isaiah 65:24, John 15:7, First Chronicles 16:11, Psalms 25:5, and Isaiah 30:15 are great scriptures to start the day with as you prepare to minister in the home.

"Part IV" is from *The Unique Woman* by Edwin Louis Cole and Nancy Corbett Cole (Tulsa: Honor Books, 1989), pp. 150-156.

PART V

A GUIDE

TO "GOLDEN RULE MANAGEMENT"

By

Mary Kay Ash

13
MARY KAY'S SECRET OF SUCCESS

This is the management philosophy that turned Mary Kay Ash's storefront cosmetics business into a multimillion dollar corporation in just twenty years. Based on the age-old Golden Rule, it encourages managers to treat staff, customers, suppliers — everyone — with the same care, consideration and concern they would like to receve themselves. It brought spectacular success to Mary Kay. Here's how it can work for you.

• **Recognize the Value of People.** People are your company's number one asset. When you treat them as you would like to be treated yourself, everyone benefits.

• **Praise Your People to Success.** Recognition is the most powerful of all motivators. Even criticism can build confidence when it's "sandwiched" between layers of praise.

• **Tear Down That Ivory Tower.** Keep all doors open. Be accessible to everyone. Remember that every good manager is also a good listener.

213

• **Be a Risk-Taker.** Don't be afraid. Encourage your people to take risks, too — and allow room for error.

• **Be Sales Oriented.** Nothing happens in business until somebody sells something. Be especially sensitive to your customers' needs and desires.

• **Be a Problem-Solver.** An effective manager knows how to recognize real problems and how to take action to solve them.

• **Create a Stress-Free Workplace.** By eliminating stress factors — fear of the boss, unreasonable deadlines, and others — you can increase and inspire productivity.

• **Develop and Promote People from Within.** Upward mobility for employees in your company builds loyalty. People give you their best when they know they'll be rewarded.

• **Keep Business in Its Proper Place.** At Mary Kay Cosmetics the order of priorities is faith, family, and career. The real key to success is creating an environment where people are encouraged to balance the many aspects of their lives.

"Part V" is from *Mary Kay on People Management* by Mary Kay Ash, copyright © 1984 by Mary Kay Cosmetics, Inc. (New York: Warner Books, Inc.), back cover.

Part VI
31-Day
DEVOTIONAL

By

John Mason

DAY 1

YOUR LEAST FAVORITE COLOR
SHOULD BE BEIGE.

Never try to defend your present position and situation. Choose to be a person who is on the offensive, not the defensive. **People who live defensively never rise above being average.** We're called, as Christians, to be on the offensive, to take the initiative. A lukewarm, indecisive person is never secure regardless of his wealth, education, or position.

Don't ever let your quest for balance become an excuse for not taking the unique, radical, invading move that God has directed you to take. Many times the attempt to maintain balance in life is really just an excuse for being lukewarm. In Joshua 1:6,7,9 the Lord says three times to Joshua, ''Be strong and courageous.'' I believe that He is saying the same thing to all believers today.

When you choose to be on the offensive, the atmosphere of your life will begin to change. So if you don't like the atmosphere of your life, choose to take the offensive position. Taking the

217

offensive is not just an action taken outside a person; it is always a decision made within.

When you do choose to be on the offensive, keep all your conflicts impersonal. Fight the issue, not the person. Speak about what God in you can do, not what others cannot do. **You will find that when all of your reasons are defensive, your cause almost never succeeds.**

Being on the offensive and taking the initiative is a master key which opens the door to opportunity in your life. Learn to create a habit of taking the initiative and **don't ever start your day in neutral.** Every morning when your feet hit the floor, you should be thinking on the offensive, reacting like an invader, taking control of your day and your life.

By pulling back and being defensive usually you enhance the problem. Intimidation always precedes defeat. If you are not sure which way to go, pray and move towards the situation in confident trust.

Be like the two fishermen who got trapped in a storm in the middle of the lake. One turned to the other and asked, "Should we pray, or should we row?" His wise companion responded, "Let's do both!"

That's taking the offensive.

Day 2

GROWTH COMES FROM BUILDING ON TALENTS, GIFTS, AND STRENGTHS — NOT BY SOLVING PROBLEMS.

One of the most neglected areas in many people's lives is the area of gifts that God has placed within them. It is amazing how some people can devote their entire lives to a field of endeavor or a profession that has nothing to do with their inborn talents. In fact, the opposite is also true. Many people spend their whole lifetime trying to change who God has made them. They ignore their God-given blessings while continually seeking to change their natural makeup. As children of God, we need to recognize our innate gifts, talents, and strengths and do everything in our power to build on them.

One good thing about God's gifts and calling is that they are permanent and enduring. Romans 11:29 tells us: ...*the gifts and calling of God are without repentance.* The Greek word translated *repentance* in this verse means "irrevocable." God cannot take away His gifts and calling in your life. **Even if you've never done anything with them, even if you've failed time and time again, God's**

219

gifts and calling are still resident within you. They are there this day, and you can choose to do something with them, beginning right now.

Gifts and talents are really God's deposits in our personal accounts, but we determine the interest on them. The greater the amount of interest and attention we give to them, the greater their value becomes. **God's gifts are never loans; they are always deposits.** As such, they are never used up or depleted. In fact, the more they are used, the greater, stronger, and more valuable they become. When they are put to good use, they provide information, insight, and revelation which cannot be received any other way or from any other source.

As Christians, we need to make full use of all the gifts and talents which God has bestowed upon us so that we do not abound in one area while becoming bankrupt in another. Someone has said, "If the only tool you have is a hammer, you tend to treat everything like a nail." Don't make that mistake; use all of the gifts God has given you. If you choose not to step out and make maximum use of the gifts and talents in your life, you will spend your days on this earth helping someone else reach his goals. Most people let others control their destiny. Don't allow anyone to take over the driver's seat in your life. Fulfill your own dreams and determine your own life's course.

Never underestimate the power of the gifts that are within you. **Gifts and talents are given us to use not only so we can fulfill to the fullest the call in our own lives, but also so we can reach the souls who are attached to those gifts.** There are people whose lives are waiting to be affected by what God has placed within you. So evaluate yourself. Define and refine your gifts, talents and strengths. Choose today to look for opportunities to exercise your unique God-endowed, God-ordained gifts and calling.

DAY 3

"THE NOSE OF THE BULLDOG IS SLANTED BACKWARDS SO HE CAN CONTINUE TO BREATHE WITHOUT LETTING GO." — WINSTON CHURCHILL

Persistent people begin their success where most others quit. We Christians need to be known as people of persistence and endurance. **One person with commitment, persistence, and endurance will accomplish more than a thousand people with interest alone.** In Hebrews 12:1 (NIV) we read: *Therefore, since we are surrounded by such a great cloud of witnesses, let us throw off everything that hinders and the sin that so easily entangles, and let us run with perseverance the race marked out for us.* The more diligently we work, the harder it is to quit. Persistence is a habit; so is quitting.

Never worry about how much money, ability, or equipment you are starting with. Just begin with a million dollars worth of determination. Remember: **it's not what you have, it's what you do with what you have that makes all the difference.** Many people eagerly begin "the good fight of faith," but they forget to add patience, persistence, and endurance to their enthusiasm. Josh Billings said: "Consider the postage stamp.

223

Its usefulness consists in the ability to stick to something until it gets there.'' You and I should be known as ''postage-stamp'' Christians.

In First Corinthians 15:58, the Apostle Paul writes: *Therefore, my beloved brethren, be ye stedfast, unmoveable, always abounding in the work of the Lord, forasmuch as ye know that your labour is not in vain in the Lord.* Peter tells us: *Wherefore, beloved, seeing that ye look for such things, be diligent that ye may be found of him in peace, without spot, and blameless* (2 Pet. 3:14). And wise Solomon points out: *Seest thou a man diligent in his business? he shall stand before kings...*(Prov. 22:29).

In the Far East the people plant a tree called the Chinese bamboo. During the first four years they water and fertilize the plant with seemingly little or no results. Then the fifth year they again apply water and fertilizer — and in five weeks' time the tree grows ninety feet in height! The obvious question is: did the Chinese bamboo tree grow ninety feet in five weeks, or did it grow ninety feet in five years? The answer is: it grew ninety feet in five years. Because if at any time during those five years the people had stopped watering and fertilizing the tree, it would have died.

Many times our dreams and plans appear not to be succeeding. We are tempted to give up and quit trying. Instead, we need to continue to water and fertilize those dreams and plans, nurturing the seeds of the vision God has placed within us. Because we know that if we do not quit, if we display perseverance and endurance, we will also reap a harvest. Charles Haddon Spurgeon said, ''By perseverance the snail reached the ark.'' We need to be like that snail.

D_{AY} 4

WE CAN GROW BY OUR QUESTIONS, AS WELL AS BY OUR ANSWERS.

Here are some important questions we should ask ourselves:

1. What one decision would I make if I knew that it would not fail?

2. What one thing should I eliminate from my life because it holds me back from reaching my full potential?

3. Am I on the path of something absolutely marvelous, or something absolutely mediocre?

4. If everyone in the United States of America were on my level of spirituality, would there be a revival in the land?

5. Does the devil know who I am?

6. Am I running from something, or to something?

7. What can I do to make better use of my time?

8. Would I recognize Jesus if I met Him on the street?

9. Who do I need to forgive?

10. What is my favorite scripture for myself, my family, my career?

11. What impossible thing am I believing and planning for?

12. What is my most prevailing thought?

13. What good thing have I previously committed myself to do that I have quit doing?

14. Of the people I respect most, what is it about them that earns my respect?

15. What would a truly creative person do in my situation?

16. What outside influences are causing me to be better or worse?

17. Can I lead anyone else to Christ?

18. In what areas do I need improvement in terms of personal development?

19. What gifts, talents, or strengths do I have?

20. What is one thing that I can do for someone else who has no opportunity to repay me?

DAY 5

DON'T ASK TIME WHERE IT'S GONE; TELL IT WHERE TO GO.

All great achievers, all successful people, are those who have been able to gain control over their time. It has been said that all human beings have been created equal in one respect: each person has been given 24 hours each day.

We need to choose to give our best time to our most challenging situation. It's not how much we do that matters; it's how much we get done. We should choose to watch our time, not our watch. One of the best timesavers is the ability to say no. Not saying no when you should is one of the biggest wastes of time you will ever experience.

Don't spend a dollar's worth of time for ten cent's worth of results.

Make sure to take care of the vulnerable times in your days. These vulnerable times are the first thing in the morning and the last thing at night. I have heard a minister say that what a person is like at midnight when he is all alone reveals that person's true self.

229

Never allow yourself to say, ''I could be doing big things if I weren't so busy doing small things!'' Take control of your time. **The greater control you exercise over your time, the greater freedom you will experience in your life.** The psalmist prayed, *So teach us to number our days, that we may apply our hearts unto wisdom* (Ps. 90:12). The Bible teaches us that the devil comes to steal, and to kill, and to destroy (John 10:10), and this verse applies to time as well as to people. The enemy desires to provide God's children with ideas of how to kill, steal, and destroy valuable time.

People are always saying, ''I'd give anything to be able to....'' There is a basic leadership principle that says, ''6 x 1 = 6.'' If you want to write a book, learn to play a musical instrument, become a better tennis player, or do anything else important, then you should devote one hour a day, six days a week, to the project. Sooner than you think, what you desire will become reality. There are not many things that a person cannot accomplish in 312 hours a year! Just a commitment of one hour a day, six days a week, is all it takes.

We all have the same amount of time each day. The difference between people is determined by what they do with the amount of time at their disposal. Don't be like the airline pilot flying over the Pacific Ocean who reported to his passengers, ''We're lost, but we're making great time!'' Remember that the future arrives an hour at a time. **Gain control of your time, and you will gain control of your life.**

DAY 6

DON'T CONSUME YOUR TOMORROWS FEEDING ON YOUR YESTERDAYS.

Decide today to get rid of any "loser's limps" which you may still be carrying from some past experience. As followers of Jesus Christ, you and I need to break the power of the past to dominate our present and determine our future.

In Luke 9:62, Jesus said, ...*No man, having put his hand to the plough, and looking back, is fit for the kingdom of God.* If we are not careful, we will allow the past to exercise a great hold on us. **The more we look backward, the less able we are to see forward.** The past makes no difference concerning what God can do for us today.

That is the beauty of the Christian life. Even when we have failed, we are able to ask for forgiveness and be totally cleansed of and released from our past actions. Whatever hold the past may have on us can be broken. It is never God Who holds us back. It is always our own choosing to allow the past to keep us from living to the fullest in the present and future. Failure is waiting around the corner for those who are living off of yesterday's successes and failures. **We should choose to be forward-focused, not past-possessed.** We should learn to profit from the past, but to invest in the future.

In Philippians 3:13,14, the Apostle Paul writes:

Brethren, I count not myself to have apprehended: but this one thing I do, forgetting those things which are behind, and reaching forth unto those things which are before,

I press toward the mark for the prize of the high calling of God in Christ Jesus.

The key here is "forgetting those things which are behind" in order to reach for "the high calling of God in Christ Jesus." To fulfill our calling in Christ, we must first forget that which lies behind. Probably the most common stronghold in a person's life is his past mistakes and failures. Today is the day to begin to shake off the shackles of the past and move forward.

The past is past. It has no life.

Day 7

THE BEST TIME OF DAY IS NOW.

Procrastination is a killer.

When you choose to kill time, you begin to kill those gifts and callings which God has placed within your life. *The Living Bible* paraphrase of Ecclesiastes 11:4 reads: *If you wait for perfect conditions, you will never get anything done.*

The first step in overcoming procrastination is to eliminate all excuses and reasons for not taking decisive and immediate action.

Everybody is on the move. They are moving forwards, backwards, or on a treadmill. The mistake most people make is thinking that the main goal of life is to stay busy. Such thinking is a trap. What is important is not whether a person is busy, but whether he is progressing. It is a question of activity versus accomplishment.

A gentleman named John Henry Fabre conducted an experiment with processionary caterpillars. They are so named because of their peculiar habit of blindly following each other no matter how they are lined up or where they are

233

going. This man took a group of these tiny creatures and did something interesting with them. He placed them in a circle. For 24 hours the caterpillars dutifully followed one another around and around. Then he did something else. He placed the caterpillars around a saucer full of pine needles (their favorite food). For six days the mindless creatures moved around and around the saucer, literally dying from starvation and exhaustion even though an abundance of choice food was located less than two inches away.

You see, they had confused activity with accomplishment.

We Christians need to be known as those who accomplish great things for God — not those who simply talk about it. Procrastinators are good at talking versus doing. It is true what Mark Twain said: ''Noise produces nothing. Often a hen who has merely laid an egg cackles as though she has laid an asteroid.''

We need to be like the apostles. They were never known much for their policies or procedures, their theories or excuses. Instead, they were known for their acts. Many people say that they are waiting for God; but in most cases God is waiting for them. We need to say with the psalmist, ''Lord, my times are in Your hands.'' (Ps. 31:15.) The price of growth is always less than the cost of stagnation. As Edmund Burke said, "The only thing necessary for the triumph of evil is for good men to do nothing."

Occasionally you may see someone who doesn't do anything, and yet seems to be successful in life. Don't be deceived. The old saying is true: "Even a broken clock is right twice a day." As Christians we are called to make progress — not excuses.

Procrastination is a primary tool of the devil to hold us back and to make us miss God's timing in our lives. *The desire of the slothful killeth him; for his hands refuse to labour* (Prov. 21:25). **The fact is, the longer we take to act on God's direction, the more unclear it becomes.**

D~AY 8

FEAR AND WORRY ARE INTEREST PAID IN ADVANCE ON SOMETHING YOU MAY NEVER OWN.

Fear is a poor chisel to carve out tomorrow. Worry is simply the triumph of fear over faith.

There's a story that is told about a woman who was standing on a street corner crying profusely. A man came up to her and asked why she was weeping. The lady shook her head and replied: ''I was just thinking that maybe someday I would get married. We would later have a beautiful baby girl. Then one day this child and I would go for a walk along this street, come to this corner, and my darling daughter would run into the street, get hit by a car, and die.''

Now that sounds like a pretty ridiculous situation — for a grown woman to be weeping her eyes out because of something that would probably never happen. Yet isn't this the way we respond when we worry? We take a situation or event which might never exist and build it up all out of proportion in our mind.

There is an old Swedish proverb that says, "Worry gives a small thing a big shadow." **Worry is simply the misuse of God's creative imagination which He has placed within each of us.** When fear rises in our mind, we should learn to expect the opposite in our life.

The word *worry* itself is derived from an Anglo-Saxon term meaning "to strangle," or "to choke off." There is no question that worry and fear in the mind does choke off the creative flow from above.

Things are seldom as they seem. "Skim milk masquerades as cream," said W.S. Gilbert. As we dwell on and worry about matters beyond our control, a negative effect begins to set in. Too much analysis always leads to paralysis. *Worry is a route which leads from somewhere to nowhere. Don't let it direct your life.*

In Psalm 55:22 the Bible says, *Cast thy burden upon the Lord, and he shall sustain thee: he shall never suffer the righteous to be moved.* Never respond out of fear, and never fear to respond. Action attacks fear; inaction builds fear.

Don't worry and don't fear. Instead, take your fear and worry to the Lord, *Casting all your care upon him; for he careth for you* (1 Pet. 5:7).

DAY 9

OUR WORDS ARE SEEDS PLANTED INTO OTHER PEOPLE'S LIVES.

What we say is important. The Bible states that out of the abundance of the heart the mouth speaks. (Matt. 12:34.) We need to change our vocabulary. We need to speak words of life and light. Our talk should always rise to the level of the Word of God.

We Christians should be known as people who speak positively, those who speak the Word of God into situations, those who speak forth words of life.

We should not be like the man who joined a monastery in which the monks were allowed to speak only two words every seven years. After the first seven years had passed, the new initiate met with the abbot who asked him, ''Well, what are your two words?''

''Food's bad,'' replied the man, who then went back to spend another seven-year period before once again meeting with his ecclesiastical superior.

''What are your two words now?'' asked the clergyman.

''Bed's hard,'' responded the man.

Seven years later — twenty-one years after his initial entry into the monastery — the man met with the abbot for the third and final time.

''And what are your two words this time?'' he was asked.

''I quit.''

''Well, I'm not surprised,'' answered the disgusted cleric, ''all you've done since you got here is complain!''

Don't be like that man; don't be known as a person whose only words are negative.

If you are a member of the ''murmuring grapevine,'' you need to resign. In John 6:43 our Lord instructed His disciples, ...*Murmur not among yourselves.* In Philippians 2:14,15 the Apostle Paul exhorted the believers of his day:

Do all things without murmurings and disputings:

That ye may be blameless and harmless, the sons of God, without rebuke, in the midst of a crooked and perverse nation, among whom ye shine as lights in the world.

Contrary to what you may have heard, talk is not cheap. Talk is very expensive. We should know that our words are powerful. What we say affects what we get from others, and what others get from us. When we speak the wrong word, it lessens our ability to see and hear the will of God.

DAY 10

VERSUS.

Every day we make decisions. Daily we are confronted with options. **We must choose one or the other.** We cannot have both. These options include:

Being bitter versus being better.

Indifference versus decisiveness.

Lukewarmness versus enthusiasm.

"If we can" versus "how we can."

"Give up" versus "get up."

Security versus risk.

Coping with evil versus overcoming evil.

Blending in versus standing out.

How much we do versus how much we get done.

Coexisting with darkness versus opposing darkness.

Destruction versus development.

Resisting versus receiving.

Complaining versus obtaining.

Trying versus committing.

Peace versus strife.

Choice versus chance.

Determination versus discouragement.

Growing versus dying.

Demanding more of ourselves versus excusing ourselves.

Doing for others versus doing for self.

Progress versus regression.

Steering versus drifting.

Priorities versus aimlessness.

Accountability versus irresponsibility.

Action versus activity.

Solutions versus problems.

More of God versus more of everything else.

Being in "Who's Who" versus asking "Why me?"

D_{AY} 11

KEEP YOUR FEET ON THE ROCK WHEN YOU REACH THE END OF YOUR ROPE.

Don't quit. There is a big difference between quitting and changing. I believe that **when God sees someone who doesn't quit, He looks down and says, ''There is someone I can use.''**

In Galatians 6:9 (NIV) we are told, *Let us not become weary in doing good, for at the proper time we will reap a harvest if we do not give up.* Look at this verse carefully. It urges us not to become weary, assuring us that we will — not might — reap a harvest if we do not give up.

God doesn't quit. It is impossible for Him to do so. In Philippians 1:6 (NIV) the Apostle Paul writes about *being confident of this, that he who began a good work in you will carry it on to completion until the day of Christ Jesus.* There are several important points in this verse. The most crucial is the fact that God does not quit. Therefore, we can have great confidence that He will complete the good work He has begun in us. He will see us through every step of the way until we have reached our ultimate destination.

One of the best scriptural examples of a person who did not quit is Joseph. He had many reasons to justify giving up. First, when he was trapped in the pit into which his brothers had thrown him because of their jealousy, I am sure he said to himself, "This is not the way I dreamed my life would work out." Later on, he had a marvelous opportunity to become discouraged and quit when he was unjustly accused and thrown into prison for a crime he did not commit. Again he could have said to himself, "This is not right; I'm not supposed to be here."

But eventually the dream which God had given Joseph became reality. He was elevated from prisoner to prime minister in one day. Although Joseph did not know or understand the steps through which the Lord would lead him, he remained true to his God. Despite the trials and obstacles he faced, he did not quit.

There is no greater reward than that which comes as a result of holding fast to the Word and will of God. Only you can decide not to lose. Most people quit right on the verge of success. Often it is right at their fingertips. There is only one degree of difference between hot water and steam.

In Luke 18 (NIV) Jesus told the parable of the persistent widow. The Bible reveals His purpose in relating this story: *Then Jesus told his disciples a parable to show them they should always pray and not give up* (v. 1). The psalmist tells us, *Commit thy way unto the Lord; trust also in him; and he shall bring it to pass* (Ps. 37:5).

The only way we can lose is to quit. That is the only decision we can make that can keep us from reaching God's goals in our lives.

DAY 12

A GOAL IS A DREAM WITH A DEADLINE.

In Habakkuk 2:2 the Lord tells the prophet, *...Write the vision, and make it plain upon tables, that he may run that readeth it.* The key to successful goal-setting is revealed in this scripture.

First, the vision must be written down. When you keep a vision in your mind, it is not really a goal; it is really nothing more than a dream. There is power in putting that dream down on paper. When you commit something to writing, commitment to achievement naturally follows. You can't start a fire with paper alone, but writing something down on paper can start a fire inside of you.

God Himself followed His Word here, by taking His vision for us and having it put down on paper in the form of the Bible. He did not just rely on the Holy Spirit to guide and direct us; He put His goals down in writing. We are told to make the word of the Lord plain upon "tables" (tablets) so that it is clear and specific as to what the vision is "...so that he may run that readeth it."

247

The key word is "run." God desires that we run with the vision and goal in our life. As long as we are running with the vision, we won't turn around. When you walk with a vision, it's easy to change directions and go the wrong way. **You can't stroll to a goal.**

In Proverbs 24:3,4 (TLB), we read: *Any enterprise is built by wise planning, becomes strong through common sense, and profits wonderfully by keeping abreast of the facts.* Simply stated, effective goal-setting and planning provides an opportunity to bring the future to the present and deal with it today. You will find that achievement is easy when your outer goals become an inner commitment.

Even though we have the Holy Spirit, we still need to prepare; we are just better equipped to do so. God's first choice for us in any situation cannot be disorder and waste of funds or resources. That's why proper planning is so important. Plan to the potential. Believe for God's biggest dream. When you plan, look to the future, not the past. You can't drive forward by looking out the rear window.

Always involve yourself with something that's bigger than you are, because that's where God is. Every great success was, at the beginning, impossible. We all have opportunity for success in our lives. It takes just as much energy and effort for a bad life as it does for a good life; yet most people live meaningless lives simply because they never decided to write their vision down and then follow through on it. Know this, if you can't see the mark, you can't press towards it.

Ponder the path of thy feet, and let all thy ways be established (Prov. 4:26). You will find that what you learn on the path to your goals is actually more valuable than achieving the goal itself. Columbus discovered America while searching for a route to India. Be on the lookout for the "Americas" in your path. Put God's vision for your life on paper, and begin to run with His plan.

Day 13

SMILE. IT ADDS TO YOUR FACE VALUE.

Christians should be the happiest, most enthusiastic, people on earth. In fact, the word *enthusiasm* comes from a Greek word, *entheous* which means "God within" or "full of God."

Smiling — being happy and enthusiastic — is always a choice and not a result. It is a decision that must be consciously made. Enthusiasm and joy and happiness will improve your personality and people's opinion of you. It will help you keep a proper perspective on life. Helen Keller said, "Keep your face to the sunshine and you cannot see the shadow."

The bigger the challenge you are facing, the more enthusiasm you need. Philippians 2:5 (NIV) says, *Your attitude should be the same as that of Christ Jesus.* I believe Jesus was a man Who had a smile on His face, a spring in His step, and joy on His countenance.

Our attitude always tells others what we expect in return.

A smile is a powerful weapon. It can even break the ice. You'll find that being happy and

251

enthusiastic is like a head cold — it's very, very contagious. A laugh a day will keep negative people away. You will also find that as enthusiasm increases, stress and fear in your life will decrease. The Bible says that the joy of the Lord is our strength. (Neh. 8:10.)

Many people say, "Well, no wonder that person is happy, confident, and positive; if I had his job and assets, I would be too." Such thinking falsely assumes that successful people are positive because they have a good income and lots of possessions. But the reverse is true. Such people probably have a good income and lots of possessions as a result of being positive, confident, and happy.

Enthusiasm always motivates to action. No significant accomplishment has ever been made without enthusiasm. In John 15:10,11 (NIV) we have a promise from the Lord, *"If you obey my commands, you will remain in my love, just as I have obeyed my Father's commands and remain in his love. I have told you this so that my joy may be in you and that your joy may be complete."*

The joy and love of the Lord are yours — so smile!

DAY 14

DON'T QUIT AFTER A VICTORY.

There are two times when a person stops: after a defeat and after a victory. Eliminating this kind of procrastination increases momentum.

Robert Schuller has a good saying: ''Don't cash in, cast into deeper water.'' Don't stop after a success, keep the forward momentum going.

One of the great prizes of victory is the opportunity to do more. The trouble is, we've innoculated ourselves with small doses of success which keep us from catching the real thing.

As I was writing this section on momentum, I couldn't get out of my mind a picture of a large boulder at the top of a hill. This boulder represents our lives. If we rock the boulder back and forth and get it moving, its momentum will make it almost unstoppable. The same is true of us.

The Bible promises us God's divine momentum in our lives. In Philippians 1:6 the Apostle Paul writes, *Being confident of this very thing, that he which hath begun a good work in you*

253

will perform it until the day of Jesus Christ. God's momentum always results in growth.

There are five ways to have divine momentum in your life:

1. Be fruitful. (2 Cor. 9:10.)

2. Speak the truth. (Eph. 4:15.)

3. Be spiritually mature. (Heb. 6:1.)

4. Crave the Word of God. (1 Pet. 2:2.)

5. Grow in the grace and knowledge of Jesus. (2 Pet. 3:18.)

God's definition of spiritual momentum is found in 2 Peter 1:5 (NIV):

For this very reason, make every effort to add to your faith goodness; and to goodness, knowledge; and to knowledge, self-control; and to self-control, perseverance; and to perseverance, godliness; and to godliness, brotherly kindness; and to brotherly kindness, love. For if you possess these qualities in increasing measure, they will keep you from being ineffective and unproductive in your knowledge of our Lord Jesus Christ.

Let go of whatever makes you stop.

DAY 15

THE MOST NATURAL THING TO DO WHEN YOU GET KNOCKED DOWN IS TO GET UP.

How we respond to failure and mistakes is one of the most important decisions we make every day. Failure doesn't mean that nothing has been accomplished. There is always the opportunity to learn something. What is in you will always be bigger than whatever is around you.

We all experience failure and make mistakes. In fact, successful people always have more failure in their lives than average people do. You will find that throughout history all great people, at some point in their lives, have failed. **Only those who do not expect anything are never disappointed. Only those who never try, never fail.** Anyone who is currently achieving anything in life is simultaneously risking failure. It is always better to fail in doing something than to excel in doing nothing. A flawed diamond is more valuable than a perfect brick. People who have no failures also have few victories.

255

Everybody gets knocked down, it's how fast he gets up that counts. There is a positive correlation between spiritual maturity and how quickly a person responds to his failures and mistakes. The greater the degree of spiritual maturity, the greater the ability to get back up and go on. The less the spiritual maturity, the longer the individual will continue to hang on to past failures. Every person knows someone who, to this day, is still held back by mistakes he made years ago. God never sees any of us as failures; He only sees us as learners.

We have only failed when we do not learn from the experience. The decision is up to us. We can choose to turn a failure into a hitching post, or a guidepost.

Here is the key to being free from the stranglehold of past failures and mistakes: learn the lesson and forget the details. Gain from the experience, but do not roll over and over in your mind the minute details of it. Build on the experience, and get on with your life.

Remember: **the call is higher than the fall.**

D_{AY} 16

THOSE WHO DON'T TAKE CHANCES DON'T MAKE ADVANCES.

All great discoveries have been made by people whose faith ran ahead of their minds. Significant achievements have not been obtained by taking small risks on unimportant issues. Don't ever waste time planning, analyzing, and risking on small ideas. It is always wise to spend more time on decisions that are irreversible and less time on those that are reversible.

Learn to stretch, to reach out where God is. Aim high and take risks. The world's approach is to look to next year based on last year. We Christians need to reach to the potential, not reckon to the past. Those who make great strides are those who take chances and plan toward the challenges of life.

Don't become so caught up in small matters that you can't take advantage of important opportunities. Most people spend their entire lives letting down buckets into empty wells. They continue to waste away their days trying to draw them up again.

Choose today to dream big, to strive to reach the full potential of your calling. Choose to major on the important issues of life, not on the unimportant. H. Stern said, "If you're hunting rabbits in tiger country, you must keep your eye peeled for tigers, but when you are hunting tigers you can ignore the rabbits." There are plenty of tigers to go around. Don't be distracted by or seek after the rabbits of life. Set your sights on "big game."

Security and opportunity are total strangers. If an undertaking doesn't include faith, it's not worthy of being called God's direction. I don't believe that God would call any of us to do anything that would not include an element of faith in Him.

There is a famous old saying that goes, "Even a turtle doesn't get ahead unless he sticks his neck out." **Dream big, because you serve a big God.**

DAY 17

YOUR BEST FRIENDS ARE THOSE WHO BRING OUT THE BEST IN YOU.

We need to be careful of the kind of insulation we use in our lives. We need to insulate ourselves from negative people and ideas. But, we should never insulate ourselves from Godly counsel and wisdom.

It is a fact that misery wants your company. In Proverbs 27:19 (TLB) we read, *A mirror reflects a man's face, but what he is really like is shown by the kind of friends he chooses.* Proverbs 13:20 tells us, *He that walketh with wise men shall be wise: but a companion of fools shall be destroyed.* We become like those with whom we associate.

Some years ago I found myself at a stagnation point in my life. I was unproductive and unable to see clearly God's direction. One day I noticed that almost all of my friends were in the same situation. When we got together, all we talked about was our problems. As I prayed about this matter, God showed me that He desired that I have "foundational-level" people in my life. Such people who bring out the best in us, those

259

who influence us to become better people ourselves. They cause us to have greater faith and confidence, to see things from God's perspective. After being with them, our spirits and our sights are raised.

I have found that **it is better to be alone than in the wrong company.** A single conversation with the right person can be more valuable than many years of study.

The Lord showed me that I needed to change my closest associations, that there were some other people I needed to have contact with on a regular basis. These were men and women of great faith, those who made me a better person just by being around them. They were the ones who saw the gifts in me and could correct me in a constructive, loving way. My choice to change my closest associations was a turning point in my life.

When you surround yourself and affiliate with the right kind of people, you enter into the God-ordained power of agreement. Ecclesiastes 4:9,10,12 (TLB) states:

Two can accomplish more than twice as much as one, for the results can be much better. If one falls, the other pulls him up; but if a man falls when he is alone, he's in trouble.

And one standing alone can be attacked and defeated, but two can stand back-to-back and conquer;

260

three is even better, for a triple-braided cord is not easily broken.

You need to steer clear of negative-thinking ''experts.'' **Remember: in the eyes of average people average is always considered outstanding.** Look carefully at the closest associations in your life, for that is the direction you are heading.

DAY 18

WE ARE CALLED TO STAND OUT, NOT BLEND IN.

A majority, many times, is a group of highly motivated snails. If a thousand people say something foolish, it's still foolish. Truth is never dependent upon consensus of opinion.

In 1 Peter 2:9, the Bible says of us Christians, *...ye are a chosen generation, a royal priesthood, an holy nation, a peculiar people; that ye should shew forth the praises of him who hath called you out of darkness into his marvellous light.*

Romans 12:2 exhorts us, *And be not conformed to this world, but be ye transformed by the renewing of your mind, that ye may prove what is that good, and acceptable, and perfect, will of God.*

One of the greatest compliments that anybody can give you is to say that you are different. We Christians live in this world, but we are aliens. We should talk differently, act differently, and perform differently. We are called to stand out.

There should be something different about you. If you don't stand out in a group, if there

263

is not something unique or different in your life, you should re-evaluate yourself.

One way to stand head and shoulders above the crowd is to choose to do regular, ordinary things in an extraordinary and supernatural way with great enthusiasm. God has always done some of His very best work through remnants, when the circumstances appear to be stacked against them. In fact, in every battle described in the Bible, God was always on the side of the "underdog," the minority.

Majority rule is not always right. It is usually those people who don't have dreams or visions of their own who want to take a vote. People in groups tend to agree on courses of action that they as individuals know are not right.

Don't be persuaded or dissuaded by group opinion. It doesn't make any difference whether anyone else believes, you must believe. **Never take direction from a crowd for your personal life. And never choose to quit just because somebody else disagrees with you.** In fact, the two worst things you can say to yourself when you get an idea is: 1) "That has never been done before," and 2) "That has been done before." Just because somebody else has gone a particular way and not succeeded does not mean that you too will fail.

Be a pioneer, catch a few arrows, and stand out.

Day 19

SAY NO TO MANY GOOD IDEAS.

One of the tricks of the devil is to get us to say yes to too many things. Then we end up being spread so thin that we are mediocre in everything and excellent in nothing.

There is one guaranteed formula for failure, and that is to try to please everyone.

There is a difference between something that is good and something that is right. Oftentimes, it is a challenge for many people to discern that which is good from that which is right. As Christians, our higher responsibility is always to do the right things. These come first. We should do the things that we're called to do, the things that are right, with excellence, first — before we start diversifying into other areas.

There comes a time in every person's life when he must learn to say no to many good ideas. In fact, the more an individual grows, the more opportunities he will have to say no. Becoming focused is a key to results. Perhaps no other virtue is so overlooked as a key to growth and success. The temptation is always to do a little bit of everything.

Saying no to a good idea doesn't always mean never. No may mean not right now.

There is power in the word *no*. No is an anointed word, one which can break the yoke of overcommitment and weakness. No can be used to turn a situation from bad to good, from wrong to right. Saying no can free you from burdens that you really don't need to carry right now.

It can also allow you to devote the correct amount of attention and effort to God's priorities in your life.

I'm sure that as you read the title of this nugget, past experiences and present situations come to mind. I'm sure you recall many situations in which no or not right now would have been the right answer. Don't put yourself through that kind of disappointment in the future.

Yes and no are the two most important words that you will ever say. These are the two words that determine your destiny in life. How and when you say them affects your entire future.

Saying no to lesser things can mean saying yes to the priorities in your life.

266

DAY 20

WHEN YOU REFUSE TO CHANGE, YOU END UP IN CHAINS.

We humans are custom-built for change.

Inanimate objects like clothes, houses, and buildings don't have the ability to truly change. They grow out of style and become unusable. But at any point in time, at any age, any one of us is able to change. To change doesn't always mean to do the opposite. In fact, most of the time, it means to add on to or slightly adjust.

When we are called upon by the Lord to change, we will continue to reach toward the same goal, but perhaps in a slightly different way. When we refuse to cooperate with the change that God is requiring of us, we make chains that constrain and restrict us.

There are three things that we know about the future: 1) it is not going to be like the past, 2) it is not going to be exactly the way we think it's going to be, and 3) the rate of change will take place faster than we imagine. The Bible indicates that in the end times in which we are now living,

267

changes will come about much quicker than ever before in history.

In 1803 the British created a civil service position in which a man was required to stand on the cliffs of Dover with a spy glass. His job was to be on the lookout for invasion. He was to ring a bell if he saw the army of Napoleon Bonaparte approaching. Now that was all well and good for the time, but that job was not eliminated until 1945! How many spy glasses on the cliffs of Dover are we still holding onto in our lives? **We should choose not to allow "the way we've always done it" to cause us to miss opportunities God is providing for us today.**

Even the most precious of all gems needs to be chiseled and faceted to achieve its best luster. There is nothing that remains so constant as change. Don't end up like concrete, all mixed up and permanently set.

In Isaiah 42:9, the Lord declares: *Behold, the former things are come to pass, and new things do I declare: before they spring forth I tell you of them.* The Bible is a book that tells us how to respond to change ahead of time. You see, I believe that we can decide in advance how we will respond to most situations. When I was coaching basketball many years ago, I used to tell my players that most situations in a game can be prepared for ahead of time. We used to practice different game situations so that when the players got into an actual game situation they would know how to respond. **One of the main reasons the Bible was written was to prepare us ahead of time, to teach us how to respond in advance to many of the situations that we will encounter in life.**

Choose to flow with God's plan. Be sensitive to the new things He is doing. Stay flexible to the Holy Spirit and know that ours is a God who directs, adjusts, moves, and corrects us. He is always working to bring us into perfection.

D_{AY} 21

"AN ARMY OF SHEEP LED BY A LION WOULD DEFEAT AN ARMY OF LIONS LED BY A SHEEP." — OLD ARAB PROVERB

What are the actions and attributes of a leader? What is it that makes him different from others?

1. A leader is always full of praise.

2. A leader learns to use the phrases "thank you" and "please" on his way to the top.

3. A leader is always growing.

4. A leader is possessed with his dreams.

5. A leader launches forth before success is certain.

6. A leader is not afraid of confrontation.

7. A leader talks about his own mistakes before talking about someone else's.

8. A leader is a person of honesty and integrity.

9. A leader has a good name.

271

10. A leader makes others better.

11. A leader is quick to praise and encourage the smallest amount of improvement.

12. A leader is genuinely interested in others.

13. A leader looks for opportunities to find someone doing something right.

14. A leader takes others up with him.

15. A leader responds to his own failures and acknowledges them before others have to discover and reveal them.

16. A leader never allows murmuring — from himself or others.

17. A leader is specific in what he expects.

18. A leaders holds accountable those who work with him.

19. A leader does what is right rather than what is popular.

20. A leader is a servant.

A leader is a lion, not a sheep.

272

DAY 22

PEOPLE ARE BORN ORIGINALS, BUT MOST DIE COPIES.

The call in your life is not a copy.

In this day of peer pressure, trends, and fads, we need to realize and accept that each person has been custom-made by God the Creator. Each of us has a unique and personal call upon our lives. We are to be our own selves and not copy other people.

Because I do a lot of work with churches, I come into contact with many different types of people. One time I talked over the phone with a pastor I had never met and who did not know me personally. We came to an agreement that I was to visit his church as a consultant. As we were closing our conversation and were setting a time to meet at the local airport, he asked me, "How will I know you when you get off the plane?"

"Oh, don't worry, pastor; I'll know you," I responded jokingly. "You all look alike."

The point of this humorous story is this: **be the person God has made YOU to be.**

273

The call of God upon our lives is the provision of God in our lives. We do not need to come up to the standards of anyone else. **The average person compares himself with others, but we Christians should always compare ourselves with the person God has called us to be.** That is our standard — God's unique plan and design for our lives. How the Lord chooses to deal with others has nothing to do with our individual call in life or God's timing and direction for us.

You and I can always find someone richer than we are, poorer than we are, or with more or less ability than we have. But how other people are, what they have, and what happens in their lives, has no effect upon our call. In Galatians 6:4 (TLB) we are admonished: *Let everyone be sure that he is doing his very best, for then he will have the personal satisfaction of work well done, and won't need to compare himself with someone else.*

God made you a certain way. You are unique. You are one of a kind. To copy others is to cheat yourself out of the fullness of what God has called you to be and to do.

So, choose to accept and become the person God has made you to be. Tap into the originality and creative genius of God in your life.

DAY 23

STOP EVERY DAY AND LOOK AT THE SIZE OF GOD.

Who is God? What is His personality like? What are His character traits?

According to the Bible, He is everlasting, just, caring, holy, divine, omniscient, omnipotent, omni-present and sovereign. He is light, perfection, abundance, salvation, wisdom, and love. He is the Creator, Savior, Deliverer, Redeemer, Provider, Healer, Advocate, and Friend. Never forget Who lives inside of you: *...the Lord...the great God, the great King above all gods* (Ps. 95:3 NIV).

John, the beloved disciple, tells us: *Ye are of God, little children, and have overcome them: because greater is he that is in you, than he that is in the world* (1 John 4:4). Period. Exclamation point. That settles it!

God and the devil are not equal, just opposite.

I travel by air quite often and one of the benefits is that every time I fly I get a glimpse of God's perspective. I like looking at my challenges

275

from 37,000 feet in the air. **No problem is too large for God's intervention, and no person is too small for God's attention.**

God is always able. If you don't need miracles, you don't need God. Dave Bordon, a friend of mine, said it best: "I don't understand the situation, but I understand God."

The miraculous realm of God always has to do with multiplication, not addition.

God likens our life in Him to seedtime and harvest. Do you realize how miraculous that is? Let me give you a conservative example: Suppose one kernel of corn produces one stalk with two ears, each ear having 200 kernels. From those 400 kernels come 400 stalks with 160,000 kernels. All from one kernel planted only one season earlier.

Our confession to the Lord should be Jeremiah 32:17 (NIV): *"Ah, Sovereign Lord, you have made the heavens and the earth by your great power and outstretched arm. Nothing is too hard for you."*

God is bigger than _____. Fill in the blank for your own life.

DAY 24

RETREAT TO ADVANCE.

Sometimes the most important and urgent thing we can do is get away to a peaceful and anointed spot.

This is one of the most powerful concepts that I personally have incorporated into my life. I'm sitting right now writing this book in a cabin up on a hill overlooking a beautiful lake, miles away from the nearest city.

As we choose to draw away for a time, we can see and hear much more clearly about how to go ahead. Jesus did this many times during His earthly life, especially just before and after major decisions. The Bible says, *...in quietness and in confidence shall be your strength...*(Is. 30:15). There's something invigorating and renewing about retreating to a quiet place of rest and peace. Silence is an environment in which great ideas are birthed.

There really are times when you should not see people, times when you should direct your whole attention toward God. I believe that every person should have a place of refuge, one out of

277

the normal scope of living, one where he can "retreat to advance" and "focus in" with just the Lord and himself.

It is important to associate intently and as often as possible with your loftiest dreams. In Isaiah 40:31 we read, *But they that wait upon the Lord shall renew their strength; they shall mount up with wings as eagles; they shall run, and not be weary; and they shall walk, and not faint.* Learn to wait upon the Lord.

Make a regular appointment with yourself; it will be one of the most important you can ever have during the course of a week or a month. Choose to retreat to advance. See how much clearer you move forward with God as a result.

DAY 25

HAVE A READY WILL AND WALK, NOT IDLE TIME AND TALK.

Acting on God's will is like riding a bicycle: if you don't go on, you go off!

Once we know God's will and timing, we should be instant to obey, taking action without delay. Delay and hesitation when God is telling us to do something now is sin. The longer we take to act on whatever God wants us to do, the more unclear His directives become. We need to make sure that we are on God's interstate highway and not in a cul-de-sac.

Ours is a God of velocity. He is a God of timing and direction. These two always go together. It is never wise to act upon only one or the other. Jumping at the first opportunity seldom leads to a happy landing. In Proverbs 25:8 the writer tells us, *Go not forth hastily to strive, lest thou know not what to do in the end thereof, when thy neighbour hath put thee to shame.* A famous saying holds that people can be divided into three groups: 1) those who make things happen, 2) those who watch things happen, and 3) those who wonder what's happening. Even the right direction taken at the wrong time is a bad decision.

Most people miss out on God's best in their lives because they're not prepared. The Bible warns us that we should be prepared continually. The Apostle Paul exhorts us: ...*be instant in season, out of season*... (2 Tim. 4:2).

There is a seasonality to God. In Ecclesiastes 3:1 we read: *To every thing there is a season, and a time to every purpose under the heaven.* Everything that you and I are involved in will have a spring (a time of planting and nurturing), a summer (a time of greatest growth), a fall (a time of harvest), and a winter (a time of decisions and planning).

Relax. Perceive, understand, and accept God's divine timing and direction.

Day 26

WHEN WISDOM REIGNS, IT POURS.

We should expect wisdom to be given to us. The Bible says in James 1:5, *If any of you lack wisdom, let him ask of God, that giveth to all men liberally, and upbraideth not; and it shall be given him.*

When you have heard God's voice, you have heard His wisdom. Thank God for His powerful wisdom. It forces a passage through the strongest barriers.

Wisdom is seeing everything from God's perspective. It is knowing when and how to use the knowledge that comes from the Lord. The old saying is true, ''He who knows nothing, doubts nothing.'' But it is also true that he who knows has a solid basis for his belief.

Just think, we human beings have available to us the wisdom of the Creator of the universe. Yet **so few drink at the fountain of His wisdom; most just rinse out their mouths.** Many may try to live without the wisdom of the bread of life, but they will die in their efforts.

281

The world doesn't spend billions of dollars for wisdom. It spends billions in search of wisdom. Yet it is readily available to everyone who seeks its divine source.

There are ten steps to gaining godly wisdom:

1. Fear God (Ps. 111:10.)

2. Please God (Eccl. 2:26.)

3. Hear God (Prov. 2:6.)

4. Look to God (Prov. 3:13.)

5. Choose God's way (Prov. 8:10,11.)

6. Be humble before God (Prov. 11:2.)

7. Take God's advice (Prov. 13:10.)

8. Receive God's correction (Prov. 29:15.)

9. Pray to God (Eph. 1:17.)

10. Know the Son of God (1 Cor. 1:30.)

DAY 27

HEARING TELLS YOU THAT THE MUSIC IS PLAYING; LISTENING TELLS YOU WHAT THE SONG IS SAYING.

One of the least developed skills among us human beings is that of listening. There are really two different kinds of listening. There is the natural listening in interaction with other people, and there is spiritual listening to the voice of God.

It has been said, "Men are born with two ears, but only one tongue, which indicates that they were meant to listen twice as much as they talk." In natural communication, leaders always "monopolize the listening." What we learn about another person will always result in a greater reward than what we tell him about ourselves. We need to learn to listen and observe aggressively. We must try harder to truly listen, and not just to hear.

In regard to spiritual listening, Proverbs 8:34,35 (NIV) quotes wisdom who says:

Blessed is the man who listens to me, watching daily at my doors, waiting at my doorway.

For whoever finds me finds life and receives favor from the Lord.

There is great wisdom and favor to be gained by listening.

Proverbs 15:31 (NIV) says, *He who listens to a life-giving rebuke will be at home among the wise.* Listening allows us to maintain a teachable spirit. It increases our "teach-ability." Those who give us a life-giving rebuke can be a great blessing to us.

The Bible teaches that we are to be quick to listen and slow to speak. (James 1:19.) We must never listen passively, especially to God. If we resist hearing, a hardening can take place in our lives. Callousness can develop. In Luke 16:31 (NIV), Jesus said of a certain group of people, *". . . 'If they do not listen to Moses and the Prophets, they will not be convinced even if someone rises from the dead.' "* The more we resist listening to the voice of God, the more hardened and less fine-tuned our hearing becomes.

There are results of spiritual hearing, as we see in Luke 8:15 (NIV). This passage relates to the parable of the sower: *". . . the seed on good soil stands for those with a noble and good heart, who hear the word, retain it, and by persevering produce a crop."* Harvest is associated not only with persevering and good seed in good soil, but also with those people who hear the Word of God and retain it.

Fine-tune your natural and spiritual ears to listen and learn.

DAY 28

GOD IS NOT YOUR PROBLEM; GOD IS ON YOUR SIDE.

Some time ago I was eating at a Mexican fast food restaurant. As I stood in line for service I noticed in front of me a very poor elderly lady who looked like a street person. When it came her turn, she ordered some water and one taco. As I sat in the booth right next to her, I couldn't help but observe and be moved with compassion toward her. Shortly after I had begun my meal I went over to her and asked if I could buy some more food for her lunch. She looked at me and angrily asked, ''Who are you?''

''Just a guy who wants to help you,'' I responded. She ignored me. I finished my meal about the same time she did, and we both got up to leave. I felt led to give her some money. In the parking lot I approached her and offered her some cash. Her only response to me was, ''Stop bothering me.'' Then, she stormed off.

Immediately, the Lord showed me that this is often the way many of us respond to Him. When He calls out to us, seeking to bless us, we act as though we don't even know Who He is. We respond to His offer of blessing by asking,'' Who are You? What do You want from me?'' The Lord, being the gracious God He is, continues to try to bless us. Yet we react by saying, ''Stop bothering me.'' We walk off, just as this lady did, missing out on the rich blessings of the Lord.

It's not the absence of problems that gives us peace; it's God's presence with us in the problems. In Matthew 28:20, Jesus sent His disciples into all the world, ordering them to preach the Gospel to every creature: *Teaching them to observe all things whatsoever I have commanded you; and, lo, I am with you alway, even unto the end of the world.* In Romans 8:38,39 (NIV), the Apostle Paul writes, *For I am convinced that neither death nor life, neither angels nor demons, neither the present nor the future, nor any powers, neither height nor depth, nor anything else in all creation, will be able to separate us from the love of God that is in Christ Jesus our Lord.* In verse 31 he declares, *What, then, shall we say in response to this? If God is for us, who can be against us?* A paraphrase might be, ''If God is for us, who cares who is against us?''

In Psalm 145:18 (NIV), we read, *The Lord is near to all who call on him, to all who call on him in truth.* James 4:8 (NIV) admonishes us, *Come near to God and he will come near to you.* In Acts 17:27

(NIV) Paul speaks: " *'For in him we live and move and have our being.'* "

Thank God that we can, without hesitation and with full confidence, lean on His eternal faithfulness.

DAY 29

LEARN THE ALPHABET FOR SUCCESS.

A Action

B Belief

C Commitment

D Direction

E Enthusiasm

F Faith

G Goals

H Happiness

I Inspiration

J Judgment

K Knowledge

L Love

M Motivation

N Nonconformity

O Obedience

P Persistence

Q Quality

R Righteousness

S Steadfastness

T Thankfulness

U Uniqueness

V Vision

W Wisdom

X (E)xcellence

Y Yieldedness

Z Zeal

DAY 30

THE MEASURE OF A WOMAN IS NOT WHAT SHE DOES ON SUNDAY, BUT RATHER WHO SHE IS MONDAY THROUGH SATURDAY.

You don't have to come out of the Spirit realm. The same closeness, strength, joy, and direction you experience on Sunday, God intends for you to walk in the rest of the week. The devil is waiting to ambush you as you leave church. He wants to bring to your mind thoughts of fear, doubt, unbelief, and destruction.

That's why we believers must guard our minds and hearts. As spiritual creatures, we walk by faith, not by sight. (2 Cor. 5:7.) We are commanded to live in the Spirit and not in the natural.

A person whose eyes, ears, and mind are directed toward the world finds it difficult to hear God speaking to him. The Lord wants to talk to you at work, at lunch, at play — everywhere you go. Some of my greatest revelations from God have come not in my prayer closet, but rather "out of the blue" in the midst of my normal, everyday life.

Our inner man is always willing, but our natural man resists. That's what Jesus meant when He said to His disciples, *Watch and pray, that ye enter not into temptation; the spirit indeed is willing, but the flesh is weak* (Matt. 26:41).

The advantage of living and walking in the Spirit is that it keeps us on the right path. In Galatians 5:16,17 (NIV) the Apostle Paul writes: *So I say, live by the Spirit, and you will not gratify the desire of the sinful nature. For the sinful nature desires what is contrary to the Spirit, and the Spirit what is contrary to the sinful nature. They are in conflict with each other, so that you do not do what you want. But if you are led by the Spirit, you are not under law.*

Thank God that our relationship with Him is not a "some-time affair," it's an "all-the-time union." In the words of the old hymn, "He leadeth me! O blessed thought!"

DAY 31

GOD WILL USE YOU
RIGHT WHERE YOU ARE TODAY.

You don't need to do anything else for God to begin to use you now. You don't have to read another paperback book, listen to another cassette tape, memorize another scripture, plant another seed gift, or repeat another creed or confession. You don't even need to attend another church service before God will begin to make use of you.

God uses willing vessels, not brimming vessels. Throughout the Bible, in order to fulfill His plans for the earth, God used many people from all walks of life. He used:

1. Matthew, a government employee, who became an apostle.

2. Gideon, a common laborer, who became a valiant leader of men.

3. Jacob, a deceiver, whose name became Israel.

4. Deborah, a housewife, who became a judge.

5. Moses, a stutterer, who became a deliverer.

6. Jeremiah, a child, who fearlessly spoke the Word of the Lord.

7. Aaron, a servant, who became God's spokesman.

8. Nicodemus, a Pharisee, who became a defender of the faith.

9. David, a shepherd boy, who became a king.

10. Hosea, a marital failure, who prophesied to save Israel.

11. Joseph, a prisoner, who became prime minister.

12. Esther, an orphan, who became a queen.

13. Elijah, a homely man, who became a mighty prophet.

14. Joshua, an assistant, who became a conqueror.

15. James and John, fishermen, who became close disciples of Christ and were known as "sons of thunder."

16. Abraham, a nomad, who became the father of many nations.

17. Peter, a businessman, who became the rock on which Christ built His Church.

18. Jacob, a refugee, who became the father of the twelve tribes of Israel.

19. John the Baptist, a vagabond, who became the forerunner of Jesus.

20. Mary, an unknown virgin, who gave birth to the Son of God.

21. Nehemiah, a cupbearer, who built the wall of Jerusalem.

22. Shadrach, Meshach, and Abednego, Hebrew exiles, who became great leaders of the nation of Babylon.

23. Hezekiah, a son of an idolatrous father, who became a king renowned for doing right in the sight of the Lord.

24. Isaiah, a man of unclean lips, who prophesied the birth of God's Messiah.

25. Paul, a persecutor, who became the greatest missionary in history and author of two-thirds of the New Testament.

All God needs to use you is all of you!

A FINAL WORD

Be the whole person God called you to be. Don't settle for anything less. Don't look back. Look forward and decide today to take steps toward His plan for your life.

And remember First Thessalonians 5:24: *Faithful is he that calleth you, who also will do it.*

"Part VI" is adapted from *An Enemy Called Average* (Tulsa: Harrison House, 1990).

PART VII
READING THE BIBLE IN ONE YEAR

A COMPLETE PROGRAM

January

1	Gen. 1-2; Ps. 1; Matt. 1-2
2	Gen. 3-4; Ps. 2; Matt. 3-4
3	Gen. 5-7; Ps. 3; Matt. 5
4	Gen. 8-9; Ps. 4; Matt. 6-7
5	Gen. 10-11; Ps. 5; Matt. 8-9
6	Gen. 12-13; Ps. 6; Matt. 10-11
7	Gen. 14-15; Ps. 7; Matt. 12
8	Gen. 16-17; Ps. 8; Matt. 13
9	Gen. 18-19; Ps. 9; Matt. 14-15
10	Gen. 20-21; Ps. 10; Matt. 16-17
11	Gen. 22-23; Ps. 11; Matt. 18
12	Gen. 24; Ps. 12; Matt. 19-20
13	Gen. 25-26; Ps. 13; Matt. 21
14	Gen. 27-28; Ps. 14; Matt. 22
15	Gen. 29-30; Ps. 15; Matt. 23
16	Gen. 31-32; Ps. 16; Matt. 24
17	Gen. 33-34; Ps. 17; Matt. 25
18	Gen. 35-36; Ps. 18, Matt. 26
19	Gen. 37-38; Ps. 19; Matt. 27
20	Gen. 39-40; Ps. 20; Matt. 28
21	Gen. 41-42; Ps. 21; Mark 1
22	Gen. 43-44; Ps. 22; Mark 2
23	Gen. 45-46; Ps. 23; Mark 3
24	Gen. 47-48; Ps. 24; Mark 4
25	Gen. 49-50; Ps. 25; Mark 5
26	Ex. 1-2; Ps. 26; Mark 6
27	Ex. 3-4; Ps. 27; Mark 7
28	Ex. 5-6; Ps. 28; Mark 8
29	Ex. 7-8; Ps. 29; Mark 9
30	Ex. 9-10; Ps. 30; Mark 10
31	Ex. 11-12; Ps. 31; Mark 11

February

1	Ex. 13-14; Ps. 32; Mark 12
2	Ex. 15-16; Ps. 33; Mark 13
3	Ex. 17-18; Ps. 34; Mark 14
4	Ex. 19-20; Ps. 35; Mark 15
5	Ex. 21-22; Ps. 36; Mark 16
6	Ex. 23-24; Ps. 37; Luke 1
7	Ex. 25-26; Ps. 38; Luke 2
8	Ex. 27-28; Ps. 39; Luke 3
9	Ex. 29-30; Ps. 40; Luke 4
10	Ex. 31-32; Ps. 41; Luke 5
11	Ex. 33-34; Ps. 42; Luke 6
12	Ex. 35-36; Ps. 43; Luke 7
13	Ex. 37-38; Ps. 44; Luke 8
14	Ex. 39-40; Ps. 45; Luke 9
15	Lev. 1-2; Ps. 46; Luke 10
16	Lev. 3-4; Ps. 47; Luke 11
17	Lev. 5-6; Ps. 48; Luke 12
18	Lev. 7-8; Ps. 49; Luke 13
19	Lev. 9-10; Ps. 50; Luke 14
20	Lev. 11-12; Ps. 51; Luke 15
21	Lev. 13; Ps. 52; Luke 16
22	Lev. 14; Ps. 53; Luke 17
23	Lev. 15-16; Ps. 54; Luke 18
24	Lev. 17-18; Ps. 55; Luke 19
25	Lev. 19-20; Ps. 56; Luke 20
26	Lev. 21-22; Ps. 57; Luke 21
27	Lev. 23-24; Ps. 58; Luke 22
28	Lev. 25
29	Lev. 59; Luke 23

March

1	Lev. 26-27; Ps. 60; Luke 24
2	Num. 1-2; Ps. 61; John 1
3	Num. 3-4; Ps. 62; John 2-3
4	Num. 5-6; Ps. 63; John 4
5	Num. 7; Ps. 64; John 5
6	Num. 8-9; Ps. 65; John 6
7	Num. 10-11; Ps. 66; John 7
8	Num. 12-13; Ps. 67; John 8
9	Num. 14-15; Ps. 68; John 9
10	Num. 16; Ps. 69; John 10
11	Num. 17-18; Ps. 70; John 11
12	Num. 19-20; Ps. 71; John 12
13	Num. 21-22; Ps. 72; John 13
14	Num. 23-24; Ps. 73; John 14-15
15	Num. 25-26; Ps. 74; John 16
16	Num. 27-28; Ps. 75; John 17
17	Num. 29-30; Ps. 76; John 18
18	Num. 31-32; Ps. 77; John 19
19	Num. 33-34; Ps. 78; John 20
20	Num. 35-36; Ps. 79; John 21
21	Deut. 1-2; Ps. 80; Acts 1
22	Deut. 3-4; Ps. 81; Acts 2
23	Deut. 5-6; Ps. 82; Acts 3-4
24	Deut. 7-8; Ps. 83; Acts 5-6
25	Deut. 9-10; Ps. 84; Acts 7
26	Deut. 11-12; Ps. 85; Acts 8
27	Deut. 13-14; Ps. 86; Acts 9
28	Deut. 15-16; Ps. 87; Acts 10
29	Deut. 17-18; Ps. 88; Acts 11-12
30	Deut. 19-20; Ps. 89; Acts 13
31	Deut. 21-22; Ps. 90; Acts 14

April

1	Deut. 23-24; Ps. 91; Acts 15
2	Deut. 25-27; Ps. 92; Acts 16
3	Deut. 28-29; Ps. 93; Acts 17
4	Deut. 30-31; Ps. 94; Acts 18
5	Deut. 32; Ps. 95; Acts 19
6	Deut. 33-34; Ps. 96; Acts 20
7	Josh. 1-2; Ps. 97; Acts 21
8	Josh. 3-4; Ps. 98; Acts 22
9	Josh. 5-6; Ps. 99; Acts 23
10	Josh. 7-8; Ps. 100; Acts 24-25
11	Josh. 9-10; Ps. 101; Acts 26
12	Josh. 11-12; Ps. 102; Acts 27
13	Josh. 13-14; Ps. 103; Acts 28
14	Josh. 15-16; Ps. 104; Rom. 1-2
15	Josh. 17-18; Ps. 105; Rom. 3-4
16	Josh. 19-20; Ps. 106; Rom. 5-6
17	Josh. 21-22; Ps. 107; Rom. 7-8
18	Josh. 23-24; Ps. 108; Rom. 9-10
19	Judg. 1-2; Ps. 109; Rom. 11-12
20	Judg. 3-4; Ps. 110; Rom. 13-14
21	Judg. 5-6; Ps. 111; Rom. 15-16
22	Judg. 7-8; Ps. 112; 1 Cor. 1-2
23	Judg. 9; Ps. 113; 1 Cor. 3-4
24	Judg. 10-11; Ps. 114; 1 Cor. 5-6
25	Judg. 12-13; Ps. 115; 1 Cor. 7
26	Judg. 14-15; Ps. 116; 1 Cor. 8-9
27	Judg. 16-17; Ps. 117; 1 Cor.10
28	Judg. 18-19; Ps. 118; 1 Cor. 11
29	Judg. 20-21; Ps. 119:1-88; 1 Cor. 12
30	Ruth 1-4; Ps. 119:89-176; 1 Cor. 13

May

1	1 Sam. 1-2; Ps. 120; 1 Cor. 14
2	1 Sam. 3-4; Ps. 121; 1 Cor. 15
3	1 Sam. 5-6; Ps. 122; 2 Cor. 16
4	1 Sam. 7-8; Ps. 123; 2 Cor. 1
5	1 Sam. 9-10; Ps. 124; 2 Cor. 2-3
6	1 Sam. 11-12; Ps. 125; 2 Cor. 4-5
7	1 Sam. 13-14; Ps. 126; 2 Cor. 6-7
8	1 Sam. 15-16; Ps. 127; 2 Cor. 8
9	1 Sam. 17; Ps. 128; 2 Cor. 9-10
10	1 Sam. 18-19; Ps. 129; 2 Cor. 11
11	1 Sam. 20-21; Ps. 130; 2 Cor. 12
12	1 Sam. 22-23; Ps. 131; 2 Cor. 13
13	1 Sam. 24-25; Ps. 132; Gal. 1-2
14	1 Sam. 26-27; Ps. 133; Gal. 3-4
15	1 Sam. 28-29; Ps. 134; Gal. 5-6
16	1 Sam. 30-31; Ps. 135; Eph. 1-2
17	2 Sam. 1-2; Ps. 136; Eph. 3-4
18	2 Sam. 3-4; Ps. 137; Eph. 5-6
19	2 Sam. 5-6; Ps. 138; Phil. 1-2
20	2 Sam. 7-8; Ps. 139; Phil. 3-4
21	2 Sam. 9-10; Ps. 140; Col. 1-2
22	2 Sam. 11-12; Ps. 141; Col. 3-4
23	2 Sam. 13-14; Ps. 142; 1 Thess. 1-2
24	2 Sam. 15-16; Ps. 143; 1 Thess. 3-4
25	2 Sam. 17-18; Ps. 144; 1 Thess. 5
26	2 Sam. 19; Ps. 145; 2 Thess. 1-3
27	2 Sam. 20-21; Ps. 146; 1 Tim. 1-2
28	2 Sam. 22; Ps. 147; 1 Tim. 3-4
29	2 Sam. 23-24; Ps. 148; 1 Tim. 5-6
30	1 Kings 1; Ps. 149; 2 Tim. 1-2
31	1 Kings 2-3; Ps. 150; 2 Tim. 3-4

June

1	1 Kings 4-5; Prov. 1; Titus 1-3
2	1 Kings 6-7; Prov. 2; Philem.
3	1 Kings 8; Prov. 3; Heb. 1-2
4	1 Kings 9-10; Prov. 4; Heb. 3-4
5	1 Kings 11-12; Prov. 5; Heb. 5-6
6	1 Kings 13-14; Prov. 6; Heb. 7-8
7	1 Kings 15-16; Prov. 7; Heb. 9-10
8	1 Kings 17-18; Prov. 8; Heb. 11
9	1 Kings 19-20; Prov. 9; Heb. 12
10	1 Kings 21-22; Prov. 10; Heb. 13
11	2 Kings 1-2; Prov. 11; James 1
12	2 Kings 3-4; Prov. 12; James 2-3
13	2 Kings 5-6; Prov. 13; James 4-5
14	2 Kings 7-8; Prov. 14; 1 Pet. 1
15	2 Kings 9-10; Prov. 15; 1 Pet. 2-3
16	2 Kings 11-12; Prov. 16; 1 Pet. 4-5
17	2 Kings 13-14; Prov. 17; 2 Pet. 1-3
18	2 Kings 15-16; Prov. 18; 1 John 1-2
19	2 Kings 17; Prov. 19; 1 John 3-4
20	2 Kings 18-19; Prov. 20; 1 John 5
21	2 Kings 20-21; Prov. 21; 2 John
22	2 Kings 22-23; Prov. 22; 3 John
23	2 Kings 24-25; Prov. 23; Jude
24	1 Chron. 1; Prov. 24; Rev. 1-2
25	1 Chron. 2-3; Prov. 25; Rev. 3-5
26	1 Chron. 4-5; Prov. 26; Rev. 6-7
27	1 Chron. 6-7; Prov. 27; Rev. 8-10
28	1 Chron. 8-9; Prov. 28; Rev. 11-12
29	1 Chron. 10-11; Prov. 29; Rev. 13-14
30	1 Chron. 12-13; Prov. 30; Rev. 15-17

July

1	1 Chron. 14-15; Prov. 31; Rev. 18-19
2	1 Chron. 16-17; Ps. 1; Rev. 20-22
3	1 Chron. 18-19; Ps. 2; Matt. 1-2
4	1 Chron. 20-21; Ps. 3; Matt. 3-4
5	1 Chron. 22-23; Ps. 4; Matt. 5
6	1 Chron. 24-25; Ps. 5; Matt. 6-7
7	1 Chron. 26-27; Ps. 6; Matt. 8-9
8	1 Chron. 28-29; Ps. 7; Matt. 10-11
9	2 Chron. 1-2; Ps. 8; Matt. 12
10	2 Chron. 3-4; Ps. 9; Matt. 13
11	2 Chron. 5-6; Ps. 10; Matt. 14-15
12	2 Chron. 7-8; Ps. 11; Matt. 16-17
13	2 Chron. 9-10; Ps. 12; Matt. 18
14	2 Chron. 11-12; Ps. 13; Matt. 19-20
15	2 Chron. 13-14; Ps. 14; Matt. 21
16	2 Chron. 15-16; Ps. 15; Matt. 22
17	2 Chron. 17-18; Ps. 16; Matt. 23
18	2 Chron. 19-20; Ps. 17; Matt. 24
19	2 Chron. 21-22; Ps. 18; Matt. 25
20	2 Chron. 23-24; Ps. 19; Matt. 26
21	2 Chron. 25-26; Ps. 20; Matt. 27
22	2 Chron. 27-28; Ps. 21; Matt. 28
23	2 Chron. 29-30; Ps. 22; Mark 1
24	2 Chron. 31-32; Ps. 23; Mark 2
25	2 Chron. 33-34; Ps. 24; Mark 3
26	2 Chron. 35-36; Ps. 25; Mark 4
27	Ezra 1-2; Ps. 26; Mark 5
28	Ezra 3-4; Ps. 27; Mark 6
29	Ezra 5-6; Ps. 28; Mark 7
30	Ezra 7-8; Ps. 29; Mark 8
31	Ezra 9-10; Ps. 30; Mark 9

August

1   Neh. 1-2; Ps. 31; Mark 10
2   Neh. 3-4; Ps. 32; Mark 11
3   Neh. 5-6; Ps. 33; Mark 12
4   Neh. 7; Ps. 34; Mark 13
5   Neh. 8-9; Ps. 35; Mark 14
6   Neh. 10-11; Ps. 36; Mark 15
7   Neh. 12-13; Ps. 37; Mark 16
8   Esth. 1-2; Ps. 38; Luke 1
9   Esth. 3-4; Ps. 39; Luke 2
10 Esth. 5-6; Ps. 40; Luke 3
11 Esth. 7-8; Ps. 41; Luke 4
12 Esth. 9-10; Ps. 42; Luke 5
13 Job 1-2; Ps. 43; Luke 6
14 Job 3-4; Ps. 44; Luke 7
15 Job 5-6; Ps. 45; Luke 8
16 Job 7-8; Ps. 46; Luke 9
17 Job 9-10; Ps. 47; Luke 10
18 Job 11-12; Ps. 48; Luke 11
19 Job 13-14; Ps. 49; Luke 12
20 Job 15-16; Ps. 50; Luke 13
21 Job 17-18; Ps. 51; Luke 14
22 Job 19-20; Ps. 52; Luke 15
23 Job 21-22; Ps. 53; Luke 16
24 Job 23-25; Ps. 54; Luke 17
25 Job 26-28; Ps. 55; Luke 18
26 Job 29-30; Ps. 56; Luke 19
27 Job 31-32; Ps. 57; Luke 20
28 Job 33-34; Ps. 58; Luke 21
29 Job 35-36; Ps. 59; Luke 22
30 Job 37-38; Ps. 60; Luke 23
31 Job 39-40; Ps. 61; Luke 24

September

1   Job 41-42; Ps. 62; John 1
2   Eccl. 1-2; Ps. 63; John 2-3
3   Eccl. 3-4; Ps. 64; John 4
4   Eccl. 5-6; Ps. 65; John 5
5   Eccl. 7-8; Ps. 66; John 6
6   Eccl. 9-10; Ps. 67; John 7
7   Eccl. 11-12; Ps. 68; John 8
8   Song of Sol. 1-2; Ps. 69; John 9
9   Song of Sol. 3-4; Ps. 70; John 10
10 Song of Sol. 5-6; Ps. 71; John 11
11 Song of Sol. 7-8; Ps. 72; John 12
12 Isaiah 1-2; Ps. 73; John 13
13 Isaiah 3-5; Ps. 74; John 14-15
14 Isaiah 6-8; Ps. 75; John 16
15 Isaiah 9-10; Ps. 76; John 17
16 Isaiah 11-13; Ps. 77; John 18
17 Isaiah 14-15; Ps. 78; John 19
18 Isaiah 16-17; Ps. 79; John 20
19 Isaiah 18-19; Ps. 80; John 21
20 Isaiah 20-22; Ps. 81; Acts 1
21 Isaiah 23-24; Ps. 82; Acts 2
22 Isaiah 25-26; Ps. 83; Acts 3-4
23 Isaiah 27-28; Ps. 84; Acts 5-6
24 Isaiah 29-30; Ps. 85; Acts 7
25 Isaiah 31-32; Ps. 86; Acts 8
26 Isaiah 33-34; Ps. 87; Acts 9
27 Isaiah 35-36; Ps. 88; Acts 10
28 Isaiah 37-38; Ps. 89; Acts 11-12
29 Isaiah 39-40; Ps. 90; Acts 13
30 Isaiah 41-42; Ps. 91; Acts 14

October

1	Isaiah 43-44; Ps. 92; Acts 15
2	Isaiah 45-46; Ps. 93; Acts 16
3	Isaiah 47-48; Ps. 94; Acts 17
4	Isaiah 49-50; Ps. 95; Acts 18
5	Isaiah 51-52; Ps. 96; Acts 19
6	Isaiah 53-54; Ps. 97; Acts 20
7	Isaiah 55-56; Ps. 98; Acts 21
8	Isaiah 57-58; Ps. 99; Acts 22
9	Isaiah 59-60; Ps. 100; Acts 23
10	Isaiah 61-62; Ps. 101; Acts 24-25
11	Isaiah 63-64; Ps. 102; Acts 26
12	Isaiah 65-66; Ps. 103; Acts 27
13	Jer. 1-2; Ps. 104; Acts 28
14	Jer. 3-4; Ps. 105; Rom. 1-2
15	Jer. 5-6; Ps. 106; Rom. 3-4
16	Jer. 7-8; Ps. 107; Rom. 5-6
17	Jer. 9-10; Ps. 108; Rom. 7-8
18	Jer. 11-12; Ps. 109; Rom. 9-10
19	Jer. 13-14; Ps. 110; Rom. 11-12
20	Jer. 15-16; Ps. 111; Rom. 13-14
21	Jer. 17-18; Ps. 112; Rom. 15-16
22	Jer. 19-20; Ps. 113; 1 Cor. 1-2
23	Jer. 21-22; Ps. 114; 1 Cor. 3-4
24	Jer. 23-24; Ps. 115; 1 Cor. 5-6
25	Jer. 25-26; Ps. 116; 1 Cor. 7
26	Jer. 27-28; Ps. 117; 1 Cor. 8-9
27	Jer. 29-30; Ps. 118; 1 Cor. 10
28	Jer. 31-32; Ps. 119:1-64; 1 Cor. 11
29	Jer. 33-34; Ps. 119:65-120; 1 Cor. 12
30	Jer. 35-36; Ps. 119:121-176; 1 Cor. 13
31	Jer. 37-38; Ps. 120; 1 Cor. 14

November

1	Jer. 39-40; Ps. 121; 1 Cor. 15
2	Jer. 41-42; Ps. 122; 1 Cor. 16
3	Jer. 43-44; Ps. 123; 2 Cor. 1
4	Jer. 45-46; Ps. 124; 2 Cor. 2-3
5	Jer. 47-48; Ps. 125; 2 Cor. 4-5
6	Jer. 49-50; Ps. 126; 2 Cor. 6-7
7	Jer. 51-52; Ps. 127; 2 Cor. 8
8	Lam. 1-2; Ps. 128; 2 Cor. 9-10
9	Lam. 3; Ps. 129; 2 Cor. 11
10	Lam. 4-5; Ps. 130; 2 Cor. 12
11	Ezek. 1-2; Ps. 131; 2 Cor. 13
12	Ezek. 3-4; Ps. 132; Gal. 1-2
13	Ezek. 5-6; Ps. 133; Gal. 3-4
14	Ezek. 7-8; Ps. 134; Gal. 5-6
15	Ezek. 9-10; Ps. 135; Eph. 1-2
16	Ezek. 11-12; Ps. 136; Eph. 3-4
17	Ezek. 13-14; Ps. 137; Eph. 5-6
18	Ezek. 15-16; Ps. 138; Phil. 1-2
19	Ezek. 17-18; Ps. 139; Phil. 3-4
20	Ezek. 19-20; Ps. 140; Col. 1-2
21	Ezek. 21-22; Ps. 141; Col. 3-4
22	Ezek. 23-24; Ps. 142; 1 Thess. 1-2
23	Ezek. 25-26; Ps. 143; 1 Thess. 3-4
24	Ezek. 27-28; Ps. 144; 1 Thess. 5
25	Ezek. 29-30; Ps. 145; 2 Thess. 1-3
26	Ezek. 31-32; Ps. 146; 1 Tim. 1-2
27	Ezek. 33-34; Ps. 147; 1 Tim. 3-4
28	Ezek. 35-36; Ps. 148; 1 Tim. 5-6
29	Ezek. 37-38; Ps. 149; 2 Tim. 1-2
30	Ezek. 39-40; Ps. 150; 2 Tim. 3-4

December

1	Ezek. 41-42; Prov. 1; Titus 1-3
2	Ezek. 43-44; Prov. 2; Philem.
3	Ezek. 45-46; Prov. 3; Heb. 1-2
4	Ezek. 47-48; Prov. 4; Heb. 3-4
5	Dan. 1-2; Prov. 5; Heb. 5-6
6	Dan. 3-4; Prov. 6; Heb. 7-8
7	Dan. 5-6; Prov. 7; Heb. 9-10
8	Dan. 7-8; Prov. 8; Heb. 11
9	Dan. 9-10; Prov. 9; Heb. 12
10	Dan. 11-12; Prov. 10; Heb. 13
11	Hos. 1-3; Prov. 11; James 1-3
12	Hos. 4-6; Prov. 12; James 4-5
13	Hos. 7-8; Prov. 13; 1 Pet. 1
14	Hos. 9-11; Prov. 14; 1 Pet. 2-3
15	Hos. 12-14; Prov. 15; 1 Pet. 4-5
16	Joel 1-3; Prov. 16; 2 Pet. 1-3
17	Amos 1-3; Prov. 17; 1 John 1-2
18	Amos 4-6; Prov. 18; 1 John 3-4
19	Amos 7-9; Prov. 19; 1 John 5
20	Obad.; Prov. 20; 2 John
21	Jonah 1-4; Prov. 21; 3 John
22	Mic. 1-4; Prov. 22; Jude
23	Mic. 5-7; Prov. 23; Rev. 1-2
24	Nah. 1-3; Prov. 24; Rev. 3-5
25	Hab. 1-3; Prov. 25; Rev. 6-7
26	Zeph. 1-3; Prov. 26; Rev. 8-10
27	Hag. 1-2; Prov. 27; Rev. 11-12
28	Zech. 1-4; Prov. 28; Rev. 13-14
29	Zech. 5-9; Prov. 29; Rev. 15-17
30	Zech. 10-14; Prov. 30; Rev. 18-19
31	Mal. 1-4; Prov. 31; Rev. 20-22

The Topical Bible Gift Series

The Mother's Topical Bible
The Father's Topical Bible
The Teen's Topical Bible
The Businessman's Topical Bible
Our Life Together
Dare To Succeed

Available from your local bookstore or from:
HONOR BOOKS • P.O. Box 55388 • Tulsa, OK 74155